Copyright © Hakimi bin Abdul Jabar (30 April 2016)

Abominable Atrocities - Reverberations of TORTURE : Omarska and Susica Concentration Camps

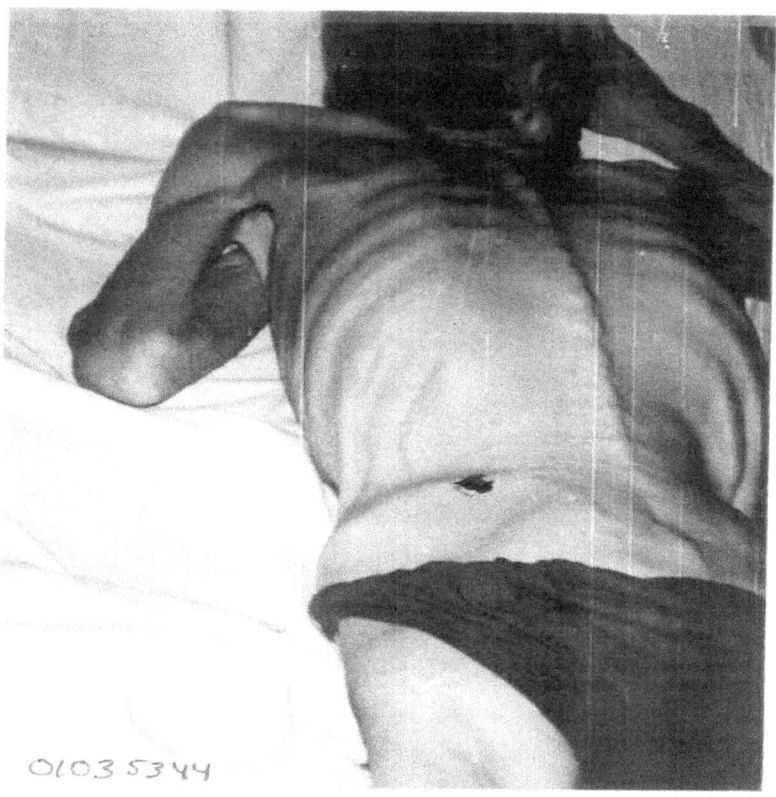

Badly beaten and emaciated Bosniak (Bosnian Muslim) man from the village of Hrnici, later died, in the Trnopolje concentration camp (Bosnian Genocide)

Contents

TORTURE

Torture (from the Latin *tortus*, "twisted") is the act of deliberately inflicting physical or psychological pain on an organism in order to fulfill some desire of the torturer or compel some action from the victim. Torture, by definition, is a knowing and intentional act; deeds which unknowingly or negligently inflict pain without a specific intent to do so are not typically considered torture.

Torture has been carried out or sanctioned by individuals, groups, and states throughout history from ancient times to modern day, and forms of torture can vary greatly in duration from only a few minutes to several days or longer. Reasons for torture can include punishment, revenge, political re-education, deterrence, interrogation or coercion of the victim or a third party, or simply the sadistic gratification of those carrying out or observing the torture. The need to torture another is thought to be the result of internal psychological pressure in the psyche of the torturer. The torturer may or may not intend to kill or injure the victim, but sometimes torture is deliberately fatal and can precede a murder or serve as a form of capital punishment. In other cases, the torturer may be indifferent to the condition of the victim. Alternatively, some forms of torture are designed to inflict psychological pain or leave as little physical injury or evidence as possible while achieving the same psychological devastation. Depending on the aim, even a form of torture that is intentionally fatal may be prolonged to allow the victim to suffer as long as possible (such as half-hanging).

Although torture was sanctioned by some states historically, it is prohibited under international law and the domestic laws of most countries, as developed in the mid-20th century. It is considered to be a violation of human rights, and is declared to be unacceptable by Article 5 of the UN Universal Declaration of Human Rights. Signatories of the Geneva Conventions of 1949 and the Additional Protocols I and II of 8 June 1977 officially agree not to torture captured persons in armed conflicts, whether international or internal. Torture is also prohibited by the United Nations Convention Against Torture, which has been ratified by 158 countries.[1] Although torture is universally condemned by all democratic nations, there have been many suspected or known instances of its sanctioned use - regardless of its legality. An example of this is the use of euphemistically-named enhanced interrogation techniques including waterboarding, known to have been used by the United States after the September 11 attacks.

National and international legal prohibitions on torture derive from a consensus that torture and similar ill-treatment are immoral, as well as impractical.[2] Despite these international conventions, organizations that monitor abuses of human rights (e.g., Amnesty International, the International Rehabilitation Council for Torture Victims, Freedom from Torture, etc.) report widespread use condoned by states in many regions of the world.[3] Amnesty International estimates that at least 81 world governments currently practice torture, some of them openly.[4] Historically, in those countries where torture was legally supported and officially condoned, wealthy patrons sponsored the creation of extraordinarily ingenious devices and techniques of torture.

UN Convention Against Torture

The United Nations Convention against Torture and Other Cruel, Inhuman or Degrading Treatment or Punishment, which is currently in force since June 26, 1987, provides a broad definition of torture. Article 1.1 of the UN Convention Against Torture reads:

For the purpose of this Convention, the term "torture" means any act by which severe pain or suffering, whether physical or mental, is intentionally inflicted on a person for such purposes as obtaining from him, or a third person, information or a confession, punishing him for an act he or a third person has committed or is suspected of having committed, or intimidating or coercing him or a third person, or for any reason based on discrimination of any kind, when such pain or suffering is inflicted by or at the instigation of or with the consent or acquiescence of a public official or other person acting in an official capacity. It does not include pain or suffering arising only from, inherent in, or incidental to, lawful sanctions.[5]

This definition was restricted to apply only to nations and to government-sponsored torture and clearly limits the torture to that perpetrated, directly or indirectly, by those acting in an official capacity, such as government personnel, law enforcement personnel, medical personnel, military personnel, or politicians. It appears to exclude:

1. torture perpetrated by gangs, hate groups, rebels, or terrorists who ignore national or international mandates;
2. random violence during war; and
3. punishment allowed by national laws, even if the punishment uses techniques similar to those used by torturers such as mutilation, whipping, or corporal punishment when practiced as lawful punishment. Some professionals in the torture rehabilitation field believe that this definition is too restrictive and that the definition of politically motivated torture should be broadened to include all acts of organized violence.[6]

Declaration of Tokyo

An even broader definition was used in the 1975 Declaration of Tokyo regarding the participation of medical professionals in acts of torture:

For the purpose of this Declaration, torture is defined as the deliberate, systematic or wanton infliction of physical or mental suffering by one or more persons acting alone or on the orders of any authority, to force another person to yield information, to make a confession, or for any other reason.[7]

This definition includes torture as part of **domestic violence** or ritualistic abuse, as well as in criminal activities.

Rome Statute of the International Criminal Court

The Rome Statute is the treaty that set up the International Criminal Court (ICC). The treaty was adopted at a diplomatic conference in Rome on 17 July 1998 and went into effect on 1 July 2002. The Rome Statute provides a simplest definition of torture regarding the prosecution of war criminals by the International Criminal Court. Paragraph 1 under Article 7(e) of the Rome Statute provides that:

"Torture" means the intentional infliction of severe pain or suffering, whether physical or mental, upon a person in the custody or under the control of the accused; except that torture shall not include pain or suffering arising only from, inherent in or incidental to, lawful sanctions.[8]

Inter-American Convention to Prevent and Punish Torture

The Inter-American Convention to Prevent and Punish Torture, which is in force since 28 February 1987, defines torture more expansively than the United Nations Convention Against Torture. Article 2 of the Inter-American Convention reads:

For the purposes of this Convention, torture shall be understood to be any act intentionally performed whereby physical or mental pain or suffering is inflicted on a person for purposes of criminal investigation, as a means of intimidation, as personal punishment, as a preventive measure, as a penalty, or for any other purpose. Torture shall also be understood to be the use of methods upon a person intended to obliterate the personality of the victim or to diminish his physical or mental capacities, even if they do not cause physical pain or mental anguish.

The concept of torture shall not include physical or mental pain or suffering that is inherent in or solely the consequence of lawful measures, provided that they do not include the performance of the acts or use of the methods referred to in this article.[9]

Amnesty International

Since 1973, Amnesty International has adopted the simplest, broadest definition of torture. It reads:

Torture is the systematic and deliberate infliction of acute pain by one person on another, or on a third person, in order to accomplish the purpose of the former against the will of the latter.[10]

Municipal level

United States

U.S. Code § 2340

Title 18 of the United States Code contains the definition of torture in 18 U.S.C. § 2340, which is only applicable to persons committing or attempting to commit torture outside of the United States.[11] It reads:

As used in this chapter—

(1) "torture" means an act committed by a person acting under the color of law specifically intended to inflict severe physical or mental pain or suffering (other than pain or suffering incidental to lawful sanctions) upon another person within his custody or physical control;

(2) "severe mental pain or suffering" means the prolonged mental harm caused by or resulting from—

(A) the intentional infliction or threatened infliction of severe physical pain or suffering;

(B) the administration or application, or threatened administration or application, of mind-altering substances or other procedures calculated to disrupt profoundly the senses or the personality;

(C) the threat of imminent death; or

(D) the threat that another person will imminently be subjected to death, severe physical pain or suffering, or the administration or application of mind-altering substances or other procedures calculated to disrupt profoundly the senses or personality; and

(3) "United States" means the several states of the United States, the District of Columbia, and the commonwealths, territories, and possessions of the United States.

> In order for the United States to assume control over this jurisdiction, the alleged offender must be a U.S. national or the alleged offender must be present in the United States, irrespective of the nationality of the victim or alleged offender. Any person who conspires to commit an offense shall be subject to the same penalties (other than the penalty of death) as the penalties prescribed for an actual act or attempting to commit an act, the commission of which was the object of the conspiracy.[11]

Torture Victim Protection Act of 1991

The Torture Victim Protection Act of 1991 provides remedies to individuals who are victims of torture by persons acting in an official capacity of any foreign nation. The definition is similar to the U.S. Code § 2340, which reads:

(b) TORTURE.—For the purposes of this Act—

(1) the term "torture" means any act, directed against an individual in the offender's custody or physical control, by which severe pain or suffering (other than pain or suffering arising only from or inherent in, or incidental to, lawful sanctions), whether physical or mental, is intentionally inflicted on that individual for such purposes as obtaining from that individual or a third person information or a confession, punishing that individual for an act that individual or a third person has committed or is suspected of having committed, intimidating or coercing that individual or a third person, or for any reason based on discrimination of any kind; and

2) mental pain or suffering refers to prolonged mental harm caused by or resulting from—

(A) the intentional infliction or threatened infliction of severe physical pain or suffering;

(B) the administration or application, or threatened administration or application, of mind altering substances or other procedures calculated to disrupt profoundly the senses or the personality;

(C) the threat of imminent death; or

(D) the threat that another individual will imminently be subjected to death, severe physical pain or suffering, or the administration or application of mind-altering substances or other procedures calculated to disrupt profoundly the senses or personality.[12]

History

In the study of the history of torture, some authorities rigidly divide the history of torture **per se** from the history of capital punishment, while noting that most forms of capital punishment are extremely painful. Torture grew into an ornate discipline, where calibrated violence served two functions: to investigate and produce confessions and to attack the body as a form of punishment. Entire populaces of towns would show up to witness an execution by torture in the public square. Those who had been "spared" torture were commonly locked barefooted into the stocks, where children took delight in rubbing feces into their hair and mouths and between their toes.[13]

Deliberately painful methods of torture and execution for severe crimes were taken for granted as part of justice until the development of Humanism in 17th century philosophy, and "cruel and unusual punishment" came to be denounced in the English Bill of Rights of 1689. The Age of Enlightenment in the western world further developed the idea of universal human rights. The adoption of the Universal Declaration of Human Rights in 1948 marks the recognition at least nominally of a general ban of torture by all UN member states.

Its effect in practice is limited, however, as the Declaration is not ratified officially and does not have legally binding character in international law, but is rather considered part of customary international law. Several countries still practice torture today. Some countries have legally codified it, and others have claimed that it is not practiced, while maintaining the use of torture in secret.[citation needed]

Since the days when Roman law prevailed throughout Europe, torture has been regarded as subtending three **classes** or **degrees** of suffering.[14] **First-degree** torture typically took the forms of whipping and beating but did not mutilate the body. The most prevalent modern example is bastinado, a technique of beating or whipping the soles of the bare feet. **Second-degree** torture consisted almost entirely of crushing devices and procedures, including exceptionally clever screw presses or "bone vises" that crushed thumbs, toes, knees, feet, even teeth and skulls in a wide variety of ways. A wide array of "boots"—machines variously, ingeniously designed to slowly squeeze feet until their bones shattered—are quite representative. Finally, **third-degree** tortures savagely mutilated the body in numerous dreadful ways, incorporating spikes, blades, boiling oil, and extremely carefully controlled fire. The serrated iron tongue shredder; the red-hot copper basin for destroying eyesight (abacination, *q.v.*); and the stocks that forcibly held the prisoner's naked feet, glistening with lard, directly over red-hot coals (foot roasting, *q.v.*) until the skin and foot muscles were burnt black and the bones fell to ashes are examples of torture in the third degree.

Antiquity[

Assyrians skinning or flaying their prisoners alive

Over time torture has been used as a means of reform, inducing public terror, interrogation, spectacle, and sadistic pleasure. The ancient Greeks and Romans used torture for interrogation. Until the 2nd century AD, torture was used only on slaves (with a few exceptions).[citation needed] After this point it began to be extended to all members of the lower classes.[citation needed] A slave's testimony was admissible *only* if extracted by torture, on the assumption that slaves could not be trusted to reveal the truth voluntarily. This torture occurred to break the bond between a master and his slave. Slaves were thought to be incapable of lying under torture.[15]

Modern scholars find the concept of torture to be compatible with society's concept of Justice during the time of the Roman Empire. Romans, Jews, Egyptians and many other cultures during that time included torture as part of their justice system. Romans had crucifixion, Jews had stoning[16] and Egyptians had desert sun death.[citation needed] All these acts of torture were considered necessary (to deter others) or good (to punish the immoral).

Middle Ages

Medieval torture rack

Torture of Christian martyrs

Medieval and early modern European courts used torture, depending on the crime of the accused and his or her social status. Torture was deemed a legitimate means to extract confessions or to obtain the names of accomplices or other information about a crime, although many confessions were greatly invalid due to the victim being forced to confess under great agony and pressure. It was permitted by law only if there was already half-proof against the accused.[18] Torture was used in continental Europe to obtain corroborating evidence in the form of a confession when other evidence already existed.[19] Often, defendants already sentenced to death would be tortured to force them to disclose the names of accomplices. Torture in the Medieval Inquisition began in 1252 with a papal bull Ad Extirpanda and ended in 1816 when another papal bull forbade its use.

A highly esteemed torture in the times of the Inquisition as a good means of interrogating "taciturn" heretics and wizards was the interrogation chair.[20]

Torture was usually conducted in secret, in underground dungeons. By contrast, torturous executions were typically public, and woodcuts of English prisoners being hanged, drawn and quartered show large crowds of spectators, as do paintings of Spanish auto-da-fé executions, in which heretics were burned at the stake. Torture was also used during this time period as a means of reform, spectacle, to induce fear into the public, and most popularly as a punishment for treason.

Medieval torture devices were varied. "They hanged them by the thumbs, or by the head, and hung fires on their feet; they put knotted strings about their heads, and writhed them so that it went to the brain ... Some they put in a chest that was short, and narrow, and shallow, and put sharp stones therein, and pressed the man therein, so that they broke all his limbs ... I neither can nor may tell all the wounds or all the tortures which they inflicted on wretched men in this land." [21] Being hung upside down, burning, crushing, breaking of limbs, and drowning were all popular medieval tortures. Specific devices were also created and used during this time, including the rack, the Pear (also mentioned in Grose's Dictionary of the Vulgar Tongue (1811) as "Choak [sic.] Pears," and described as being "formerly used in Holland."), thumbscrews, animals like rats, the iron chair, and the cat o nine tails.[22]

Early modern period

Lingchi – execution by slow slicing – in Beijing around 1904.

During the early modern period, the torture of witches took place. In 1613, Anton Praetorius described the situation of the prisoners in the dungeons in his book *Gründlicher Bericht Von Zauberey und Zauberern* (*Thorough Report about Sorcery and Sorcerers*). He was one of the first to protest against all means of torture.

While secular courts often treated suspects ferociously, Will and Ariel Durant argued in *The Age of Faith* that many of the most vicious procedures were inflicted upon pious heretics by even more pious friars. The Dominicans gained a reputation as some of the most fearsomely innovative torturers in medieval Spain.

Torture was continued by Protestants during the Renaissance against teachers who they viewed as heretics. In 1547 John Calvin had Jacques Gruet arrested in Geneva, Switzerland. Under torture he confessed to several crimes including writing an anonymous letter left in the pulpit which threatened death to Calvin and his associates.[23] The Council of Geneva had him beheaded with Calvin's approval.[24][25][26][27] Suspected witches were also tortured and burnt by Protestant leaders, though more often they were banished from the city, as well as suspected spreaders of the plague, which was considered a more serious crime.[28]

In England the trial by jury developed considerable freedom in evaluating evidence and condemning on circumstantial evidence, making torture to extort confessions unnecessary. For this reason in England a regularized system of judicial torture never existed and its use was limited to political cases. Torture was in theory not permitted under English law, but in Tudor and early Stuart times, under certain conditions, torture was used in England. For example, the confession of Marc Smeaton at the trial of Anne Boleyn was presented in written form only, either to hide from the court that Smeaton had been tortured on the rack for four hours, or because Thomas Cromwell was worried that he would recant his confession if cross-examined. When Guy Fawkes was arrested for his role in the Gunpowder Plot of 1605 he was tortured until he revealed all he knew about the plot. This was not so much to extract a confession, which was not needed to prove his guilt, but to extract from him the names of his fellow conspirators. By this time torture was not routine in England and a special warrant from King James I was needed before he could be tortured. The wording of the warrant shows some concerns for humanitarian considerations, the severity of the methods of interrogation were to be increased gradually until the interrogators were sure that Fawkes had told all he knew. In the end this did not help Fawkes much as he was broken on the only rack in England, which was in the Tower of London.

The privy council attempted to have John Felton who stabbed George Villiers, 1st Duke of Buckingham to death in 1628 questioned under torture on the rack, but the judges resisted, unanimously declaring its use to be contrary to the laws of England.[29] Torture was abolished in England around 1640 (except *peine forte et dure*, which was abolished in 1772).

In Colonial America, women were sentenced to the stocks with wooden clips on their tongues or subjected to the "dunking stool" for the gender-specific crime of talking too much.[30] Certain Native American peoples, especially in the area that later became the eastern half of the United States, engaged in the sacrificial torture of war captives.[31]

In the 17th century the number of incidents of judicial torture decreased in many European regions. Johann Graefe in 1624 published *Tribunal Reformation*, a case against torture. Cesare Beccaria, an Italian lawyer, published in 1764 "An Essay on Crimes and Punishments", in which he argued that torture unjustly punished the innocent and should be unnecessary in proving guilt. Voltaire (1694–1778) also fiercely condemned torture in some of his essays.

While in Egypt in 1798, Napoleon Bonaparte wrote to Major-General Berthier regarding the validity of torture as an interrogation tool:

The barbarous custom of whipping men suspected of having important secrets to reveal must be abolished. It has always been recognized that this method of interrogation, by putting men to the torture, is useless. The wretches say whatever comes into their heads and whatever they think one wants to believe. Consequently, the Commander-in-Chief forbids the use of a method which is contrary to reason and humanity.[32]

European states abolished torture from their statutory law in the late 18th and early 19th centuries. England abolished torture in about 1640 (except peine forte et dure, which England only abolished in 1772), Scotland in 1708, Prussia in 1740, Denmark around 1770, Russia in 1774, Austria and Polish-Lithuanian Commonwealth in 1776, Italy in 1786, France in 1789, and Baden in 1831.[33][34][35] Sweden was the first to do so in 1722 and the Netherlands did the same in 1798. Bavaria abolished torture in 1806 andWürttemberg in 1809. In Spain, the Napoleonic conquest put an end to torture in 1808. Norway abolished it in 1819 and Portugal in 1826. The last European jurisdictions to abolish legal torture were Portugal (1828) and the canton of Glarus in Switzerland (1851).[36]

Native Americans scalping and torturing prisoners, published in May 1873

Tortures included the chevalet, in which an accused witch sat on a pointed metal horse with weights strung from her feet.[37] Sexual humiliation torture included forced sitting on red-hot stools.[38] Gresillons, also called pennywinkis in Scotland, or pilliwinks, crushed the tips of fingers and toes in a vise-like device.[39] The Spanish Boot, or "leg-screw", used mostly in Germany and Scotland, was a steel boot that was placed over the leg of the accused and was tightened. The pressure from the squeezing of the boot would break the shin bone in pieces. An anonymous Scotsman called it "The most severe and cruel pain in the world".[40] Ingenious variants of the Spanish boot were also designed to slowly crush feet between iron plates armed with terrifying spikes. The echelle more commonly known as the "ladder" or "rack" was a long table that the accused would lie upon and be stretched violently. The torture was used so intensely that on many occasions the victim's limbs would be pulled out of the socket and, at times, the limbs would even be torn from the body entirely. On some special occasions a tortillon was used in conjunction with the ladder which would severely squeeze and mutilate the genitals at the same time as the stretching was occurring.[39] Similar to the ladder was the "lift". It too stretched the limbs of the accused, this time however the victim's feet were strapped to the ground and their arms were tied behind their back before a rope was tied to their hands and lifted upwards. This caused the arms to break before the horrific portion of the stretching began.[40] Finally, the judicial system of King James favored the use of the turkas, an ingenious iron instrument for destroying fingernails and toenails. The sharp point of the instrument was first pushed under the nail to the root, splitting the nail down the centerline. Pincers then grabbed either edge of the destroyed nail and slowly, very slowly, tore it from the finger or toe.

Since 1948

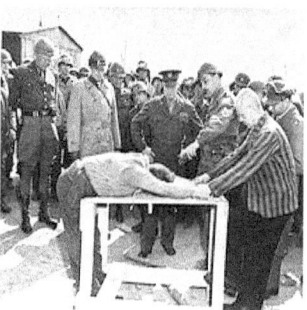

Survivors of the Ohrdruf concentration camp demonstrate torture methods used in the camp

Red Terror: Polish Captain Rosinski, tortured by Bolsheviks in the Polish–Soviet War, 1920

Main article: Use of torture since 1948

Modern sensibilities have been shaped by a profound reaction to the war crimes and crimes against humanity committed by the Axis Powers and Allied Powers in the Second World War, which have led to a sweeping international rejection of most if not all aspects of the practice.[41] Even as many states engage in torture, few wish to be described as doing so, either to their own citizens or to the international community. A variety of devices bridge this gap, including state denial, "secret police", "need to know", a denial that given treatments are torturous in nature, appeal to various laws (national or international), the use of jurisdictional argument and the claim of "overriding need". Throughout history and today, many states have engaged in torture, albeit unofficially. Torture ranges from physical, psychological, political, interrogations techniques, and also includes rape of anyone outside of law enforcement.[42]

According to scholar Ervand Abrahamian, although there were several decades of prohibition of torture that spread from Europe to most parts of the world, by the 1980s, the taboo against torture was broken and torture "returned with a vengeance," propelled in part by television and an opportunity to break political prisoners and broadcast the resulting public recantations of their political beliefs for "ideological warfare, political mobilization, and the need to win 'hearts and minds.'"[43] In the years 2004 and 2005, over 16 countries were documented using torture.[44] In an attempt to bring global awareness, Human Rights Watch, has created an internet site to alert people to news and multimedia publications about torture occurring worldwide.[44] The International Rehabilitation Council for Torture Victims [IRCT] made a global analysis of torture based on [Amnesty International, 2001], [Human Rights Watch, 2003], [United Nations, 2002], [U.S. Department of State, 2002] yearly human rights reports. These reports showed that torture and ill treatment are consistently report based on all four sources in 32 countries. At least two reports the use of torture and ill treatment in at least 80 countries. These reports confirm the assumption that torture occurs in a quarter of the world's countries on a regular basis. This global prevalence of torture is estimated on the magnitude of particular high-risk groups and the amount of torture used by these groups. "Such groups comprise refugees and persons who are or have been under torture." [42] According to professor Darius Rejali, although dictatorships may have used tortured "more, and more indiscriminately", it was modern democracies, "the United States, Britain, and France" who "pioneered and exported techniques that have become the lingua franca of modern torture: methods that leave no marks."[45] The practice of torture used as the oppression against political opponents or could be a part of criminal investigation or interrogation techniques in order to obtain the desired information and keep law enforcement empowered over everyday citizens.[42]

The modern concept of torture methods that leave no physical evidence is noted in 1995 by the Diagnostic and Statistical Manual of Mental Disorders DSM-IV within the changing definition of Post-traumatic Stress Disorder PTSD. This revised definition included psychological torture stating: "Expresses concern that the Diagnostic and Statistical Manual of Mental Disorders definition of posttraumatic stress disorder does not include those forms of psychological torture in which the physical integrity of a person is not threatened. It is suggested that any diagnostic criterion that characterizes the traumatic stressors leading to PTSD should be expressed in such a way that psychological forms of torture are included."[46] After 1995, the sweeping definition of changes from 'any act by which severe pain or suffering, whether *mental* or *physical*,is intentionally inflicted on a person' to including the terms *psychological torture* and including examples such as,interrogation techniques range from sleep deprivation, solitary confinement, fear and humiliation to severe sexual and cultural humiliation and use of threats and phobias to induce fear of death or injury.[47]

Torture still occurs in liberal democracies despite several international treaties such as the International Covenant on Civil and Political Rights and the UN Convention Against Torture making torture illegal. Despite such international conventions, torture cases continue to arise such as the 2004 Abu Ghraib torture and prisoner abuse scandal committed by personnel of the United States Army. The U.S. Constitution and U.S. law prohibits the use of torture, yet such human rights violations occurred during the War on Terror under the euphemism Enhanced interrogation. The United States has revised the previous torture policy in 2009 under the Obama Administration. This revision revokes the Executive Order 13440 of July 20, 2007, under which the incident at Abu Ghraib and prisoner abuse occurred. Executive Order 13491 of January 22, 2009 further defines United States policy on torture and interrogation techniques in an attempt to further prevent another torture incident.[48]

According to the findings of Dr. Christian Davenport of the University of Notre Dame, Professor William Moore of Florida State University, and David Armstrong of Oxford University during their torture research, evidence suggests that non-governmental organizations have played the most determinant factor for stopping torture once it gets started.[49] Preliminary research suggests that it is civil society, not government institutions, that can stop torture once it has begun. Due to this inability to control abuse and torture in society creates an imperfect Democracy and compliance with internationally agreed upon standards for civil and political rights.[42] Organizations such as Amnesty International serve to expose widespread human rights violations and hold the individuals accountable to the international community.

Laws against torture[edit]

On 10 December 1948, the United Nations General Assembly adopted the Universal Declaration of Human Rights (UDHR). Article 5 states, "No one shall be subjected to torture or to cruel, inhuman or degrading treatment or punishment."[60] Since that time, a number of other international treaties have been adopted to prevent the use of torture. The most notable treaties relating to torture are the United Nations Convention Against Torture and the Geneva Conventions of 1949 and their Additional Protocols I and II of 8 June 1977.[61]

United Nations Convention Against Torture

The United Nations Convention against Torture and Other Cruel, Inhuman or Degrading Treatment or Punishment came into force in June 1987. The most relevant articles are Articles 1, 2, 3, and 16.

Article 1

1. For the purposes of this Convention, the term "torture" means any act by which severe pain or suffering, whether physical or mental, is intentionally inflicted on a person for such purposes as obtaining from him or a third person information or a confession, punishing him for an act he or a third person has committed or is suspected of having committed, or intimidating or coercing him or a third person, or for any reason based on discrimination of any kind, when such pain or suffering is inflicted by or at the instigation of or with the consent or acquiescence of a public official or other person acting in an official capacity. It does not include pain or suffering arising only from, inherent in or incidental to lawful sanctions.
2. This article is without prejudice to any international instrument or national legislation which does or may contain provisions of wider application.

Article 2

1. Each State Party shall take effective legislative, administrative, judicial or other measures to prevent acts of torture in any territory under its jurisdiction.
2. No exceptional circumstances whatsoever, whether a state of war or a threat of war, internal political instability or any other public emergency, may be invoked as a justification of torture.
3. An order from a superior officer or a public authority may not be invoked as a justification of torture.

Article 3

1. No State Party shall expel, return ("refouler") or extradite a person to another State where there are substantial grounds for believing that he would be in danger of being subjected to torture.

2. For the purpose of determining whether there are such grounds, the competent authorities shall take into account all relevant considerations including, where applicable, the existence in the State concerned of a consistent pattern of gross, flagrant or mass violations of human rights.

Article 16

1. Each State Party shall undertake to prevent in any territory under its jurisdiction other acts of cruel, inhuman or degrading treatment or punishment which do not amount to torture as defined in article I, when such acts are committed by or at the instigation of or with the consent or acquiescence of a public official or other person acting in an official capacity. In particular, the obligations contained in articles 10, 11, 12 and 13 shall apply with the substitution for references to torture of references to other forms of cruel, inhuman or degrading treatment or punishment.

2. The provisions of this Convention are without prejudice to the provisions of any other international instrument or national law which prohibits cruel, inhuman or degrading treatment or punishment or which relates to extradition or expulsion.

Map of the world with parties to the United Nations Convention Against Torture shaded dark green, states that have signed but not ratified the treaty in light green, and non-parties in gray

Note several points:

- Article 1: Torture is "severe pain or suffering".[62] The European Court of Human Rights (ECHR) influences discussions on this area of international law. See the section Other conventions for more details on the ECHR ruling.
- Article 2: There are "no exceptional circumstances whatsoever where a state can use torture and not break its treaty obligations."[63]
- Article 16: Obliges signatories to prevent "acts of cruel, inhuman or degrading treatment or punishment", in all territories under their jurisdiction.

Optional Protocol to the UN Convention Against Torture

The Optional Protocol to the Convention Against Torture (OPCAT) entered into force on 22 June 2006 as an important addition to the UNCAT. As stated in Article 1, the purpose of the protocol is to "establish a system of regular visits undertaken by independent international and national bodies to places where people are deprived of their liberty, in order to prevent torture and other cruel, inhuman or degrading treatment or punishment."[64] Each state ratifying the OPCAT, according to Article 17, is responsible for creating or maintaining at least one independent national preventive mechanism for torture prevention at the domestic level.

Rome Statute of the International Criminal Court

Map of the world with the states parties to the International Criminal Court (as of May 2013) shown in green, states that have signed but not ratified the treaty in orange, and non-parties in gray

Main article: International Criminal Court

The Rome Statute, which established the International Criminal Court (ICC), provides for criminal prosecution of individuals responsible for genocide, war crimes, and crimes against humanity. The statute defines torture as "intentional infliction of severe pain or suffering, whether physical or mental, upon a person in the custody or under the control of the accused; except that torture shall not include pain or suffering arising only from, inherent in or incidental to, lawful sanctions". Under Article 7 of the statute, torture may be considered a crime against humanity "when committed as part of a widespread or systematic attack directed against any civilian population, with knowledge of the attack".[65] Article 8 of the statute provides that torture may also, under certain circumstances, be prosecuted as a war crime.[66]

The ICC came into existence on 1 July 2002[67] and can only prosecute crimes committed on or after that date.[68] The court can generally exercise jurisdiction only in cases where the accused is a national of a state party to the Rome Statute, the alleged crime took place on the territory of a state party, or a situation is referred to the court by the United Nations Security Council.[69] The court is designed to complement existing national judicial systems: it can exercise its jurisdiction only when national courts are unwilling or unable to investigate or prosecute such crimes.[70] Primary responsibility to investigate and punish crimes is therefore reserved to individual states.

Geneva Conventions

The four Geneva Conventions provide protection for people who fall into enemy hands. The conventions do not clearly divide people into combatant and non-combatant roles. The conventions refer to:

- "wounded and sick combatants or non-combatants"
- "civilian persons who take no part in hostilities, and who, while they reside in the zones, perform no work of a military character"[72]
- "Members of the armed forces of a Party to the conflict as well as members of militias or volunteer corps forming part of such armed forces"
- "Members of other militias and members of other volunteer corps, including those of organized resistance movements belonging to a Party to the conflict and operating in or outside their own territory, even if this territory is occupied"
- "Members of regular armed forces who profess allegiance to a government or an authority not recognized by the Detaining Power"
- "Persons who accompany the armed forces without actually being members thereof, such as civilian members of military aircraft crews, war correspondents, supply contractors, members of labour units or of services responsible for the welfare of the armed forces"
- "Members of crews, including masters, pilots and apprentices, of the merchant marine and the crews of civil aircraft of the Parties to the conflict"
- "Inhabitants of a non-occupied territory, who on the approach of the enemy spontaneously take up arms to resist the invading forces, without having had time to form themselves into regular armed units".[73]

The first (GCI), second (GCII), third (GCIII), and fourth (GCIV) Geneva Conventions are the four most relevant for the treatment of the victims of conflicts. All treaties states in Article 3, in similar wording, that in a non-international armed conflict, "Persons taking no active part in the hostilities, including members of armed forces who have laid down their arms... shall in all circumstances be treated humanely." The treaty also states that there must not be any "violence to life and person, in particular murder of all kinds, mutilation, cruel treatment and torture" or "outrages upon personal dignity, in particular humiliating and degrading treatment".[74][75][76][77]

GCI covers wounded combatants in an international armed conflict. Under Article 12, members of the armed forces who are sick or wounded "shall be respected and protected in all circumstances. They shall be treated humanely and cared for by the Party to the conflict in whose power they may be, without any adverse distinction founded on sex, race, nationality, religion, political opinions, or any other similar criteria. Any attempts upon their lives, or violence to their persons, shall be strictly prohibited; in particular, they shall not be murdered or exterminated, subjected to torture or to biological experiments".

GCII covers shipwreck survivors at sea in an international armed conflict. Under Article 12, persons "who are at sea and who are wounded, sick or shipwrecked, shall be respected and protected in all circumstances, it being understood that the term "shipwreck" means shipwreck from any cause and includes forced landings at sea by or from aircraft. Such persons shall be treated humanely and cared for by the Parties to the conflict in whose power they may be, without any adverse distinction founded on sex, race, nationality, religion, political opinions, or any other similar criteria. Any attempts upon their lives, or violence to their persons, shall be strictly prohibited; in particular, they shall not be murdered or exterminated, subjected to torture or to biological experiments".

GCIII covers the treatment of **prisoners of war** (POWs) in an international armed conflict. In particular, Article 17 says that "No physical or mental torture, nor any other form of coercion, may be inflicted on prisoners of war to secure from them information of any kind whatever. Prisoners of war who refuse to answer may not be threatened, insulted or exposed to unpleasant or disadvantageous treatment of any kind." POW status under GCIII has far fewer exemptions than "Protected Person" status under GCIV. Captured combatants in an international armed conflict automatically have the protection of GCIII and are POWs under GCIII unless they are determined by a competent tribunal to not be a POW (GCIII Article 5).

GCIV covers most **civilians** in an international armed conflict, and says they are usually "Protected Persons" (see exemptions section immediately after this for those who are not). Under Article 32, civilians have the right to protection from "murder, torture, corporal punishments, mutilation and medical or scientific experiments...but also to any other measures of brutality whether applied by civilian or military agents."

Geneva Convention IV exemptions

GCIV provides an important exemption:

Where in the territory of a Party to the conflict, the latter is satisfied that an individual protected person is definitely suspected of or engaged in activities hostile to the security of the State, such individual person shall not be entitled to claim such rights and privileges under the present Convention [ie GCIV] as would ... be prejudicial to the security of such State ... In each case, such persons shall nevertheless be treated with humanity (GCIV Article 5)

Also, nationals of a State not bound by the Convention are not protected by it, and nationals of a neutral State in the territory of a combatant State, and nationals of a co-belligerent State, cannot claim the protection of GCIV if their home state has normal diplomatic representation in the

State that holds them (Article 4), as their diplomatic representatives can take steps to protect them. The requirement to treat persons with "humanity" implies that it is still prohibited to torture individuals not protected by the Convention.

The George W. Bush administration afforded fewer protections, under GCIII, to detainees in the "War on Terror" by codifying the legal status of an "unlawful combatant". If there is a question of whether a person is a lawful combatant, he (or she) must be treated as a POW "until their status has been determined by a competent tribunal" (GCIII Article 5). If the tribunal decides that he is an unlawful combatant, he is not considered a protected person under GCIII. However, if he is a protected person under GCIV he still has some protection under GCIV, and must be "treated with humanity and, in case of trial, shall not be deprived of the rights of fair and regular trial prescribed by the present Convention" (GCIV Article 5).[nb 3]

Additional Protocols to the Geneva Conventions

There are two additional protocols to the Geneva Convention: Protocol I (1977), relating to the protection of victims of international armed conflicts and Protocol II (1977), relating to the protection of victims of non-international armed conflicts. These clarify and extend the definitions in some areas, but to date many countries, including the United States, have either not signed them or have not ratified them.

Protocol I does not mention torture but it does affect the treatment of POWs and Protected Persons. In Article 5, the protocol explicitly involves "the appointment of Protecting Powers and of their substitute" to monitor that the Parties to the conflict are enforcing the Conventions.[78] The protocol also broadens the definition of a lawful combatant in wars against "alien occupation, colonial domination and racist regimes" to include those who carry arms openly but are not wearing uniforms, so that they are now lawful combatants and protected by the Geneva Conventions—although only if the Occupying Power has ratified Protocol I. Under the original conventions, combatants without a recognizable insignia could be treated as war criminals, and potentially be executed. It also mentions spies, and defines who is a mercenary. Mercenaries and spies are considered an unlawful combatant, and not protected by the same conventions.

Protocol II "develops and supplements Article 3 [relating to the protection of victims of non-international armed conflicts] common to the Geneva Conventions of 12 August 1949 without modifying its existing conditions of application" (Article 1). Any person who does not take part in or ceased to take part in hostilities is entitled to humane treatment. Among the acts prohibited against these persons are, "Violence to the life, health and physical or mental well-being of persons, in particular murder as well as cruel treatment such as torture, mutilation or any form of corporal punishment" (Article 4.a). "Outrages upon personal dignity, in particular humiliating and degrading treatment, rape, enforced prostitution and any form of indecent assault" (Article 4.e), and "Threats to commit any of the foregoing acts" (Article 4.h).[79] Clauses in other articles implore humane treatment of enemy personnel in an internal conflict. These have a bearing on torture, but no other clauses explicitly mention torture.

Other conventions

In accordance with the optional UN Standard Minimum Rules for the Treatment of Prisoners (1955), *"corporal punishment, punishment by placing in a dark cell, and all cruel, inhuman or degrading punishments shall be completely prohibited as punishments for disciplinary offences."*[80] The International Covenant on Civil and Political Rights, (16 December 1966), explicitly prohibits torture and *"cruel, inhuman or degrading treatment or punishment"* by signatories.[81]

European agreements

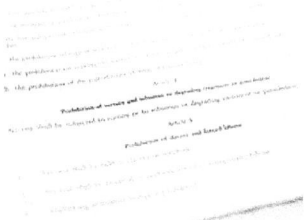

Article 4 of the Charter of Fundamental Rights of the European Union prohibits torture.

In 1950 during the Cold War, the participating member states of the Council of Europe signed the European Convention on Human Rights. The treaty was based on the UDHR. It included the provision for a court to interpret the treaty, and Article 3 **"Prohibition of torture"** stated; *"No one shall be subjected to torture or to inhuman or degrading treatment or punishment."*[82]

In 1978, the European Court of Human Rights ruled that the five techniques of "sensory deprivation" were not torture as laid out in Article 3 of the European Convention on Human Rights, but were *"inhuman or degrading treatment"*[83] (see Accusations of use of torture by United Kingdom for details). This case occurred nine years before the United Nations Convention Against Torture came into force and had an influence on thinking about what constitutes torture ever since.[84]

On 26 November 1987, the member states of the Council of Europe, meeting at Strasbourg, adopted the European Convention for the Prevention of Torture and Inhuman or Degrading Treatment or Punishment (ECPT). Two additional Protocols amended the Convention, which entered into force on 1 March 2002. The Convention set up the Committee for the Prevention of Torture to oversee compliance with its provisions.

Inter-American Convention

The Inter-American Convention to Prevent and Punish Torture, currently ratified by 18 nations of the Americas and in force since 28 February 1987, defines torture more expansively than the United Nations Convention Against Torture.

For the purposes of this Convention, torture shall be understood to be any act intentionally performed whereby physical or mental pain or suffering is inflicted on a person for purposes of criminal investigation, as a means of intimidation, as personal punishment, as a preventive measure, as a penalty, or for any other purpose. Torture shall also be understood to be the use of methods upon a person intended to obliterate the personality of the victim or to diminish his physical or mental capacities, even if they do not cause physical pain or mental anguish.

The concept of torture shall not include physical or mental pain or suffering that is inherent in or solely the consequence of lawful measures, provided that they do not include the performance of the acts or use of the methods referred to in this article.[9]

Supervision of anti-torture treaties

The Istanbul Protocol, an official UN document, is the first set of international guidelines for documentation of torture and its consequences. It became a United Nations official document in 1999.

Under the provisions of OPCAT that entered into force on 22 June 2006 independent international and national bodies regularly visit places where people are deprived of their liberty, to prevent torture and other cruel, inhuman or degrading treatment or punishment. Each state that ratified the OPCAT, according to Article 17, is responsible for creating or maintaining at least one independent national preventative mechanism for torture prevention at the domestic level.

The European Committee for the Prevention of Torture, citing Article 1 of the European Convention for the Prevention of Torture, states that it will, "by means of visits, examine the treatment of persons deprived of their liberty with a view to strengthening, if necessary, the protection of such persons from torture and from inhuman or degrading treatment or punishment".[85]

In times of armed conflict between a signatory of the Geneva Conventions and another party, delegates of the International Committee of the Red Cross (ICRC) monitor the compliance of signatories to the Geneva Conventions, which includes monitoring the use of torture. Human rights organizations, such as Amnesty International, the World Organization Against Torture, and Association for the Prevention of Torture work actively to stop the use of torture throughout the world and publish reports on any activities they consider to be torture.[86]

Municipal law

States that ratified the United Nations Convention Against Torture have a treaty obligation to include the provisions into municipal law. The laws of many states therefore formally prohibit torture. However, such *de jure* legal provisions are by no means a proof that, *de facto*, the signatory country does not use torture. To prevent torture, many legal systems have a right against self-incrimination or explicitly prohibit undue force when dealing with suspects.

The French 1789 Declaration of the Rights of Man and of the Citizen, of constitutional value, prohibits submitting suspects to any hardship not necessary to secure his or her person.

The U.S. Constitution and U.S. law prohibits the use of unwarranted force or coercion against any person who is subject to interrogation, detention, or arrest. The Fifth Amendment to the United States Constitution includes protection against self-incrimination, which states that "[n]o person...shall be compelled in any criminal case to be a witness against himself". This serves as the basis of the Miranda warning, which U.S. law enforcement personnel issue to individuals upon their arrest. Additionally, the U.S. Constitution's Eighth Amendment forbids the use of "cruel and unusual punishments," which is widely interpreted as prohibiting torture. Finally, 18 U.S.C. § 2340[87] *et seq.* define and forbid torture committed by U.S. nationals outside the United States or non-U.S. nationals who are present in the United States. As the United States recognizes customary international law, or the law of nations, the U.S. Alien Tort Claims Act and the Torture Victim Protection Act also provides legal remedies for victims of torture outside of the United States. Specifically, the status of torturers under the law of the United States, as determined by a famous legal decision in 1980, Filártiga v. Peña-Irala, 630 F.2d 876 (1980), is that, "the torturer has become, like the pirate and the slave trader before him, hostis humani generis, an enemy of all mankind."[88]

Exclusion of evidence obtained under torture

International law

Article 15 of the 1984 United Nations Convention Against Torture specify that:

Each State Party shall ensure that any statement which is established to have been made as a result of torture shall not be invoked as evidence in any proceedings, except against a person accused of torture as evidence that the statement was made.

A similar provision is also found in Article 10 of the 1985 Inter-American Convention to Prevent and Punish Torture:

No statement that is verified as having been obtained through torture shall be admissible as evidence in a legal proceeding, except in a legal action taken against a person or persons accused of having elicited it through acts of torture, and only as evidence that the accused obtained such statement by such means.

These provisions have the double dissuasive effect of nullifying any utility in using torture with the purpose of eliciting confession, as well as confirming that should a person extract statements by torture, this can be used against him or her in criminal proceedings.[89] The reason for this because experience has shown that under torture, or even under a threat of torture, a person will say or do anything solely to avoid the pain. As a result, there is no way to know whether or not the resulting statement is actually correct. If any court relies on any evidence obtained from torture regardless of validity, it provides an incentive for state officials to force a confession, creating a marketplace for torture, both domestically and overseas.[90]

Within national borders

Most states have prohibit their legal systems from accepting evidence that is extracted by torture. The question of the use of evidence obtained under torture has arisen in connection with prosecutions during the War on Terror in the United Kingdom and the United States.

United Kingdom

In September 2011, United Kingdom involvement in torture overseas was brought to light with the unearthing of top secret documents by Human Rights Watch in Libya. Chief Executive of Freedom from Torture Keith Best stated: 'If verified, they show the head of counter-terrorism at MI6 engaged in fawning dialogue with Gaddafi's former intelligence chief, Musa Kusa, about how "glad" Britain was to help deliver into his hands the Libyan dissident Abdel Hakim Belhadj' on Freedom from Torture website. During a House of Commons debate on 7 July 2009, MP David Davis accused the UK government of outsourcing torture, by allowing Rangzieb Ahmed to leave the country (even though they had evidence against him upon which he was later convicted for terrorism) to Pakistan, where it is said the Inter-Services Intelligence was given the go ahead by the British intelligence agencies to torture Ahmed. Davis further accused the government of trying to gag Ahmed, stopping him coming forward with his accusations, after he had been imprisoned back in the UK. He said, there was "an alleged request to drop his allegations of torture: if he did that, they could get his sentence cut and possibly give him some money. If this request to drop the torture case is true, it is frankly monstrous. It would at the very least be a criminal misuse of the powers and funds under the Government's Contest strategy, and at worst a conspiracy to pervert the course of justice."[91]

In 2003, the United Kingdom's Ambassador to Uzbekistan, Craig Murray, suggested that it was "wrong to use information gleaned from torture".[92] The unanimous Law Lords judgment on 8 December 2005 confirmed this position. They ruled that, under English law tradition, "torture and its fruits" could not be used in court.[93] But the information thus obtained could be used by the British police and security services as "it would be ludicrous for them to disregard information about a ticking bomb if it had been procured by torture."[94] The Law Lords thus dismissed concerns about the validity of information obtained under torture, which have been expressed by various security agents and human rights activists.

Murray's accusations did not lead to any investigation by his employer, the FCO, and he resigned after disciplinary action was taken against him in 2004. The Foreign and Commonwealth Office itself is being investigated by the National Audit Office because of accusations that it has victimized, bullied and intimidated its own staff.[95]

Murray later stated that he felt that he had unwittingly stumbled upon what has been called "torture by proxy".[96] He thought that Western countries moved people to regimes and nations where it was known that information would be extracted by torture, and made available to them.[citation needed]

Murray states that he was aware from August 2002 "that the CIA were bringing in detainees to Tashkent from Bagram airport Afghanistan, who were handed over to the Uzbek security services (SNB). I presumed at the time that these were all Uzbek nationals — that may have been a false presumption. I knew that the CIA were obtaining intelligence from their subsequent interrogation by the SNB." He goes on to say that he did not know at the time that any non-Uzbek nationals were flown to Uzbekistan and although he has studied the reports by several journalists and finds their reports credible he is not a firsthand authority on this issue.[97]

United States

In May 2008, Susan J. Crawford, the official overseeing prosecutions before the Guantanamo military commissions, declined to refer for trial the case of Mohammed al-Qahtanibecause she said, "we tortured [him]."[98][99] Crawford said that a combination of techniques with clear medical consequences amounted to the legal definition of torture, and that torture "tainted everything going forward."[98]

On October 28, 2008, Guantanamo military judge Stephen R. Henley ruled that the government cannot use statements made as a result of torture in the military commission case against Afghan national Mohammed Jawad. The judge held that Jawad's alleged confession to throwing a grenade at two U.S. service members and an Afghan interpreter was obtained after armed Afghan officials on December 17, 2002,[100] threatened to kill Jawad and his family. The government had previously told the judge that Jawad's alleged confession while in Afghan custody was central to the case against him. Hina Shamsi, staff attorney with the American Civil Liberties Union National Security Project stated: "We welcome the judge's decision that death threats constitute torture and that evidence obtained as a result must be excluded from trial. Unfortunately, evidence obtained through torture and coercion is pervasive in military commission cases that, by design, disregard the most fundamental due process rights, and no single decision can cure that."[101] A month later, on November 19, the judge again rejected evidence gathered through coercive interrogations in the military commission case against Afghan national Mohammed Jawad, holding that the evidence collected while Jawad was in U.S. custody on December 17–18, 2002, cannot be admitted in his trial,[102] mainly because the U.S. interrogator had blindfolded and hooded Jawad in order to frighten him.[103]

In the 2010 New York trial of Ahmed Khalfan Ghailani who was accused of complicity in the 1998 bombings of U.S. embassies in Tanzania and Kenya, Judge Lewis A. Kaplanruled evidence obtained under coercion inadmissible.[104] The ruling excluded an important witness, whose name had been extracted from the defendant under duress.[105] The jury acquitted him of 280 charges and convicted on only one charge of conspiracy.[104][105]

Aspects
Ethical arguments

Main article: Ethical arguments regarding torture

Picture of Satar Jabar, one of the prisoners subjected to torture at Abu Ghraib. He was *not* in Abu Ghraib on charges of terrorism, as was commonly believed, but rather for carjacking.

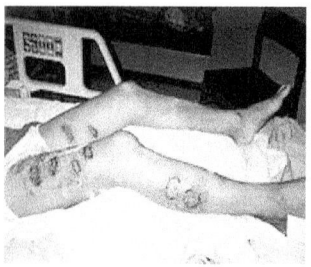

Falun Gong practitioner, tortured by guards in a labor camp in the Boluo Area of China (PRC)

Torture has been criticized on humanitarian and moral grounds, on the grounds that evidence extracted by torture is unreliable, and because torture corrupts institutions that tolerate it.[106] Besides degrading the victim, torture debases the torturer: American advisors alarmed at torture by their South Vietnamese allies early in the Vietnam War concluded that "if a commander allowed his officers and men to fall in to these vices [they] would pursue them for their own sake, for the perverse pleasure they drew from them."[107] The consequent degeneracy destroyed discipline and morale: "[a] soldier had to learn that he existed to uphold law and order, not to undermine it."[107]

Organizations like Amnesty International argue that the universal legal prohibition is based on a universal philosophical consensus that torture and ill-treatment are repugnant, abhorrent, and immoral.[108] But since shortly after the September 11, 2001 attacks there has been a debate in the United States about whether torture is justified in some circumstances. Some people, such as Alan M. Dershowitz and Mirko Bagaric, have argued the need for information outweighs the moral and ethical arguments against torture.[109][110] However, after coercive practices were banned, interrogators in Iraq saw an increase of 50 percent more high-value intelligence. Maj. Gen. Geoffrey D. Miller, the American commander in charge of detentions and interrogations, stated "*a rapport-based interrogation that recognizes respect and dignity, and having very well-trained interrogators, is the basis by which you develop intelligence rapidly and increase the validity of that intelligence.*"[111] Others including Robert Mueller, FBI Director since 5 July 2001, have pointed out that despite former Bush Administration claims that waterboarding has "disrupted a number of attacks, maybe dozens of attacks", they do not believe that evidence gained by the U.S. government through what supporters of the techniques call "enhanced interrogation" has disrupted a single attack and no one has come up with a documented example of lives saved thanks to these techniques.[112][113] On 19 June 2009, the US government announced that it was delaying the scheduled release of declassified portions of a report by the CIA Inspector General that reportedly cast doubt on the effectiveness of the "enhanced interrogation" techniques employed by CIA interrogators, according to references to the report contained in several Bush-era Justice Department memos declassified in the Spring of 2009 by the US Justice Department.[114][115][116]

The ticking time bomb scenario, a thought experiment, asks what to do to a captured terrorist who has placed a nuclear bomb in a populated area. If the terrorist is tortured, he may explain how to defuse the bomb. The scenario asks if it is ethical to torture the terrorist. A 2006 BBC poll held in 25 nations gauged support for each of the following positions:[117]

- Terrorists pose such an extreme threat that governments should be allowed to use some degree of torture if it may gain information that saves innocent lives.
- Clear rules against torture should be maintained because any use of torture is immoral and will weaken international human rights.

An average of 59% of people worldwide rejected torture. However, there was a clear divide between those countries with strong rejection of torture (such as Italy, where only 14% supported torture) and nations where rejection was less strong. Often this lessened rejection is found in countries severely and frequently threatened by terrorist attacks. E.g., Israel, despite its Supreme Court outlawing torture in 1999, showed 43% supporting torture, but 48% opposing, India showed 37% supporting torture and only 23% opposing.[118]

Within nations there is a clear divide between the positions of members of different ethnic groups, religions, and political affiliations, sometimes reflecting distinctions between groups considering themselves threatened or victimized by terror acts and those from the alleged perpetrator groups. For example, the study found that among Jews in Israel 53% favored some degree of torture and only 39% wanted strong rules against torture while Muslims in Israel were overwhelmingly against any use of torture, unlike Muslims polled elsewhere. Differences in general political views also can matter. In one 2006 survey by the Scripps Center at Ohio University, 66% of Americans who identified themselves as strongly Republican supported torture, compared to 24% of those who identified themselves as strongly Democratic.[119] In a 2005 U.S. survey 72% of American Catholics supported the use of torture in some circumstances compared to 51% of American secularists.[120] A Pew survey in 2009 similarly found that the religiously unaffiliated are the least likely (40 percent) to support torture, and that the more a person claims to attend church, the more likely he or she is to condone torture; among racial/religious groups, white evangelical Protestants were far and away the most likely (62 percent) to support inflicting pain as a tool of interrogation.

Demonstration of <u>waterboarding</u> at a street protest during a visit by <u>Condoleezza Rice</u> to <u>Iceland</u>, May 2008

A *Today/Gallup poll* "found that sizable majorities of Americans disagree with tactics ranging from leaving prisoners naked and chained in uncomfortable positions for hours, to trying to make a prisoner think he was being drowned".[122]

There are also different attitudes as to what constitutes torture, as revealed in an ABC News/Washington Post poll, where more than half of the Americans polled thought that techniques such as <u>sleep deprivation</u> were not torture.[123]

In practice, so-called "enhanced interrogation" techniques were employed by the CIA in situations that did not involve the "ticking time bomb" scenario that has been the subject of opinion polls and public debate. In April 2009 a former senior U.S. intelligence official and a former Army psychiatrist stated that the Bush administration applied pressure on interrogators to use the "enhanced interrogation" techniques on detainees to find evidence of cooperation between al Qaida and the late Iraqi dictator Saddam Hussein's regime.[124] The purported <u>link between al Qaida and Hussein's regime</u>, which has been disproven,[125] was a key political justification for the <u>Iraq War</u>. On 13 May 2009, former NBC News investigative producer Robert Windrem reported, as confirmed by former Iraq Survey Group leader <u>Charles Duelfer</u>, that the Vice President's Office suggested that an interrogation team led by Duelfer waterboard an Iraqi prisoner suspected of knowing about a relationship between al Qaeda and Saddam.[126][127]

On 14 February 2010, in an appearance on <u>ABC</u>'s <u>This Week</u>, Vice-President <u>Dick Cheney</u> reiterated his support of <u>waterboarding</u> and "<u>enhanced interrogation</u>" techniques for captured terrorist suspects, saying, "I was and remain a strong proponent of our enhanced interrogation program."[128]

Pressed by the BBC in 2010 on his personal view of waterboarding, Presidential Advisor <u>Karl Rove</u> said: "I'm proud that we kept the world safer than it was, by the use of these techniques. They're appropriate, they're in conformity with our international requirements and with US law."[129]

A 15-month investigation by the Guardian and BBC Arabic, published on March 2013, disclosed that "the US sent a veteran of the *dirty wars* in Central America to oversee Iraqicommando units involved in acts of torture during the American-led occupation. These American citizens could theoretically be tried by the International Criminal Court even though the US is not a signatory. But it would have to be referred by the UN security council and, given that the US has a veto on the council, this hypothesis is very improbable."Reprieve Legal Director Kat Craig said: "This latest exposé of human rights abuses shows that torture is endemic to US foreign policy; these are considered and deliberate acts, not only sanctioned but developed by the highest echelons of US security service."[130]

Utilitarian arguments against torture[edit]

There is a strong utilitarian argument against torture; namely, that there is simply no scientific evidence supporting its effectiveness.[131]

The lack of scientific basis for the effectiveness of torture as an interrogation techniques is summarized in a 2006 Intelligence Science Board report titled "EDUCING INFORMATION, Interrogation: Science and Art, Foundations for the Future".[132]

On the other hand, some have pointed to some specific cases where torture has elicited true information.[133]

Rejection[edit]

A famous example of rejection of the use of torture was cited by the Argentine National Commission on the Disappearance of Persons in whose report, Italian general Carlo Alberto Dalla Chiesa was reputed to have said in connection with the investigation of the disappearance of prime minister Aldo Moro, "Italy can survive the loss of Aldo Moro. It would not survive the introduction of torture."[134]

Secrecy[edit]

Before the emergence of modern policing, torture was an important aspect of policing and the use of it was openly sanctioned and acknowledged by the authority. The Economist magazine proposed that one of the reasons torture endures is that torture does indeed work in some instances to extract information/confession, if those who are being tortured are indeed guilty.[135] Depending on the culture, torture has at times been carried on in silence (official silence [136]), semi-silence (known but not spoken about), or openly acknowledged in public (to instill fear and obedience).

In the 21st century, even when states sanction their interrogation methods, torturers often work outside the law. For this reason, some prefer methods that, while unpleasant, leave victims alive and unmarked. A victim with no visible damage may lack credibility when telling tales of torture, whereas a person missing fingernails or eyes can easily prove claims of torture. Mental torture, however can leave scars just as deep and long-lasting as physical torture.[137] Professional torturers in some countries have used techniques such as electrical shock, asphyxiation, heat, cold, noise, and sleep deprivation, which leave little evidence, although in other contexts torture frequently results in horrific mutilation or death. However the most common and prevalent form of torture worldwide in both developed and under-developed countries is beating.[138]

Methods and devices[edit]

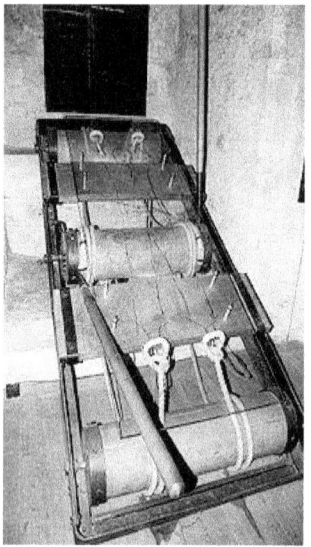

A rack in the Tower of London.

The contrast shown between Guy Fawkes' signatures: the one above (a faint, shaky 'Guido') was done immediately after torture; the one below eight days later.[139]

Main article: List of torture methods and devices

Psychological torture uses non-physical methods that cause psychological suffering. Its effects are not immediately apparent unless they alter the behavior of the tortured person. Since there is no international political consensus on what constitutes psychological torture, it is often overlooked, denied, and referred to by different names.[citation needed]

Psychological torture is less well known than physical torture and tends to be subtle and much easier to conceal. In practice the distinctions between physical and psychological torture are often blurred.[citation needed] Physical torture is the inflicting of severe pain or suffering on a person. In contrast, psychological torture is directed at the psyche with calculated violations of psychological needs, along with deep damage to psychological structures and the breakage of beliefs underpinning normal sanity. Torturers often inflict both types of torture in combination to compound the associated effects.[citation needed]

Psychological torture also includes deliberate use of extreme stressors and situations such as mock execution, shunning, violation of deep-seated social or sexual norms and taboos, or extended solitary confinement. Because psychological torture needs no physical violence to be effective, it is possible to induce severe psychological pain, suffering, and trauma with no externally visible effects.[citation needed]

Rape and other forms of sexual abuse are often used as methods of torture for interrogative or punitive purposes.[140]

In medical torture, medical practitioners use torture to judge what victims can endure, to apply treatments that enhance torture, or act as torturers in their own right. Josef Mengele and Shirō Ishii were infamous during and after World War II for their involvement in medical torture and murder. In recent years, however, there has been a push to end medical complicity in torture through both international and state-based legal strategies, as well as litigations against individual physicians.[141]

Pharmacological torture is the use of drugs to produce psychological or physical pain or discomfort. Tickle torture is an unusual form of torture which nevertheless has been documented, and can be both physically and psychologically painful.[142][143][144][145]

Murder[edit]

Torture murder involves torture to the point of murder as for punishment in law enforcement agencies of countries that allow torture.Murderers might also torture their victims to death for sadistic reasons. Some terrorist groups tortures—typically commencing with the forcible extraction of all ten fingernails, all ten toenails, and all thirty-two teeth—before executing them by such barbaric techniques as slow decapitation via butcher knife.[citation needed] Ancient conceptual forerunners of torture murder include drawing and quartering andflaying.

Effects[edit]

The consequences of torture reach far beyond immediate pain. Many victims suffer from post-traumatic stress disorder (PTSD), which includes symptoms such as flashbacks (or intrusive thoughts), severe anxiety, insomnia, nightmares, depression and memory lapses. Torture victims often feel guilt and shame, triggered by the humiliation they have endured. Many feel that they have betrayed themselves or their friends and family. All such symptoms are normal human responses to abnormal and inhuman treatment.[146]

Organizations like Freedom from Torture and the Center for Victims of Torture try to help survivors of torture obtain medical treatment and to gain forensic medical evidence to obtain political asylum in a safe country and/or to prosecute the perpetrators.

Torture is often difficult to prove, particularly when some time has passed between the event and a medical examination, or when the torturers are immune from prosecution. Many torturers around the world use methods designed to have a maximum psychological impact while leaving only minimal physical traces. Medical and Human Rights Organizations worldwide have collaborated to produce the Istanbul Protocol, a document designed to outline common torture methods, consequences of torture, and medico-legal examination techniques. Typically deaths due to torture are shown in an autopsy as being due to "natural causes" like heart attack, inflammation, or embolism due to extreme stress.[147]

For survivors, torture often leads to lasting mental and physical health problems.

Physical problems can be wide-ranging, e.g. sexually transmitted diseases, musculo-skeletal problems, brain injury, post-traumatic epilepsy and dementia or chronic pain syndromes.

Mental health problems are equally wide-ranging; common are post-traumatic stress disorder, depression and anxiety disorder. Psychic deadness, erasure of intersubjectivity, refusal of meaning-making, perversion of agency, and an inability to bear desire constitute the core features of the post-traumatic psychic landscape of torture.[148]

The most terrible, intractable, legacy of torture is the killing of desire - that is, of curiosity, of the impulse for connection and meaning-making, of the capacity for mutuality, of the tolerance for ambiguity and ambivalence. For these patients, to know another mind is unbearable. To connect with another is irrelevant. They are entrapped in what was born(e) during their trauma, as they perpetuate the erasure of meaning, re-enact the dynamics of annihilation through sadomasochistic, narcissistic, paranoid, or self-deadening modes of relating, and mobilize their agency toward warding off mutuality, goodness, hope and connection. In brief, they live to prove death. And it is this perversion of agency and desire that constitutes the deepest post-traumatic injury, and the most invisible and pernicious of human-rights violations.[148]

On 19 August 2007, the **American Psychology Association** (APA) voted to bar participation, to intervene to stop, and to report involvement in a wide variety of interrogation techniques as torture, including "using **mock executions**, simulated drowning, sexual and religious humiliation, stress positions or sleep deprivation", as well as "the exploitation of prisoners' phobias, the use of mind-altering drugs, **hooding**, forced nakedness, the use of dogs to frighten detainees, exposing prisoners to extreme heat and cold, physical assault and threatening the use of such techniques against a prisoner or a prisoner's family."[149]

However, the APA rejected a stronger resolution that sought to prohibit "all psychologist involvement, either direct or indirect, in any interrogations at U.S. detention centers for foreign detainees or citizens detained outside normal legal channels." That resolution would have placed the APA alongside the American Medical Association and the American Psychiatric Association in limiting professional involvement in such settings to direct patient care. The APA echoed the Bush administration by condemning isolation, sleep deprivation, and sensory deprivation or over-stimulation only when they are likely to cause lasting harm.

Psychiatric treatment of torture-related medical problems might require a wide range of expertise and often specialized experience. Common treatments are **psychotropicmedication**, e.g. **SSRI** **antidepressants**, **counseling**, **Cognitive Behavioural Therapy**, **family systems therapy** and **physiotherapy**.

*See **Psychology of torture** for psychological impact, and aftermath, of torture.*

Rehabilitation[edit]

The aim of rehabilitation is to empower the torture victim to resume as full a life as possible. Rebuilding the life of someone whose dignity has been destroyed takes time and as a result long-term material, medical, psychological and social support is needed.[150]

Treatment must be a coordinated effort that covers both physical and psychological aspects. It is important to take into consideration the patients' needs, problems, expectations, views and cultural references.[150]

The consequences of torture are likely to be influenced by many internal and external factors. Therefore, rehabilitation needs to employ different treatment approaches, taking into account the victims' individual needs, as well as the cultural, social and political environment.[150]

Rehabilitation centres around the world, notably the members of the **International Rehabilitation Council for Torture Victims**, commonly offer multi-disciplinary support and counselling, including:

- medical attention / psychotherapeutic treatment
- psychosocial support / trauma treatment
- legal services and redress
- social reintegration.

In the case of asylum seekers and refugees, the services may also include assisting in documentation of torture for the asylum decision, language classes and help in finding somewhere to live and work.[150]

Rehabilitation of secondary survivors[edit]

In the worst case, torture can affect several generations. The physical and mental after-effects of torture often place great strain on the entire family and society. Children are particularly vulnerable. They often suffer from feelings of guilt or personal responsibility for what has happened. Therefore, other members of the survivor's family – in particular the spouse and children – are also offered treatment and counselling.[150]

Broken societies[edit]

In some instances, whole societies can be more or less traumatized where torture has been used in a systematic and widespread manner. In general, after years of repression,conflict and war, regular support networks and structures have often been broken or destroyed.[150]

Providing psychosocial support and redress to survivors of torture and trauma can help reconstruct broken societies.[151] "Rehabilitation centres therefore play a key role in promoting democracy, co-existence and respect for human rights. They provide support and hope, and act as a symbol of triumph over the manmade terror of torture which can hold back the development of democracy of entire societies."[150]

See also[edit]

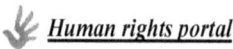 *Human rights portal*

- Abu Ghraib torture and prisoner abuse
- Capital punishment
- Center for Victims of Torture
- Civil rights
- Counter-insurgency
- *Death by a Thousand Cuts*
- Enhanced interrogation techniques

- Famine
- Freedom from Torture
- Genocide
- Human Rights
- International Rehabilitation Council for Torture Victims
- Peine forte et dure
- Physicians for Human Rights
- Political violence
- Program for Torture Victims
- Psychology of torture
- Rehabilitation and Research Centre for Torture Victims
- Torture (journal)
- Torture trade
- UN International Day in Support of Victims of Torture
- War
- World Organisation Against Torture

Notes[edit]

Footnotes

1. **Jump up^** When ratifying the treaty the United States added a reservation that the definition of "cruel, inhuman or degrading treatment or punishment" meant "the cruel, unusual and inhumane treatment or punishment prohibited by the Fifth, Eighth, and/or Fourteenth Amendments to the Constitution of the United States."(Yee, Sienho (2004). *International crime and punishment: selected issues*, University Press of America, ISBN 0-7618-2887-7,ISBN 978-0-7618-2887-7 p. 208, Footnote 18. cites *Convention Against Torture*, Annex I,I.). See also Torture and the United States.
2. **Jump up^** The unanimous Law Lords judgment on 8 December 2005 ruled that, under English law tradition, "torture and its fruits" could not be used in court (Torture evidence inadmissible in UK courts, Lords rules by Staff and agencies in The Guardian 8 December 2005). But the information thus obtained could be used by the British police and security services as "it would be ludicrous for them to disregard information about a ticking bomb if it had been procured by torture." (Torture ruling's international impact by Jon Silverman BBC 8 December 2005)
3. **Jump up^** "Every person in enemy hands must have some status under international law: he is either a prisoner of war and, as such, covered by the Third Convention, a civilian covered by the Fourth Convention, or again, a member of the medical personnel of the armed forces who is covered by the First Convention. *There is no* intermediate status; nobody in enemy hands can be outside the law. We feel

that this is a satisfactory solution – not only satisfying to the mind, but also, and above all, satisfactory from the humanitarian point of view.", because in the opinion of the ICRC "If civilians directly engage in hostilities, they are considered 'unlawful' or 'unprivileged' combatants or belligerents (the treaties of humanitarian law do not expressly contain these terms). They may be prosecuted under the domestic law of the detaining state for such action" (Jean Pictet (ed.) – Commentary: IV Geneva Convention Relative to the Protection of Civilian Persons in Time of War (1958) – 1994 reprint edition). Geneva Conventions Protocol I Article 51.3 also covers this interpretation "Civilians shall enjoy the protection afforded by this section, unless and for such time as they take a direct part in hostilities".

Citations

1. **Jump up^** *"United Nations Treaty Collection"*. *United Nations. Retrieved 7 October 2010.*

2. **Jump up^** *"Torture and Ill-Treatment in the 'War on Terror'"*. *Amnesty International. 1 November 2005. Retrieved 22 October 2008.*

3. **Jump up^** Amnesty International Report 2005 Report 2006 Archived 18 July 2015 at the Wayback Machine.

4. **Jump up^** *"Report 08: At a Glance"*. *Amnesty International. 2008. Archived from the original on 8 July 2008. Retrieved 22 October 2008.*

5. **Jump up^** *"A/RES/39/46. Convention against Torture and Other Cruel, Inhuman or Degrading Treatment or Punishment"*. un.org.

6. **Jump up^** James Jaranson, "The Science and Politics of Rehabilitating Torture Survivors," in *Caring for Victims of Torture*, edited by Michael K. Popkin, Amer Psychiatric Pub Inc.1998.

7. **Jump up^** World Medical Association, *Declaration of Tokyo, 1975.*

8. **Jump up^** ROME STATUTE OF THE INTERNATIONAL CRIMINAL COURT, INTERNATIONAL CRIMINAL COURT, 17 July 1998.

9. ^ Jump up to:[a][b] Inter-American Convention to Prevent and Punish Torture. Organization of American States, 9 December 1985.

10. **Jump up^** Amnesty International, (1973) *Torture in the Eighties*. USA Edition. Amnesty International Publication. Archived 2 May 2015 at the Wayback Machine.

11. ^ Jump up to:[a][b] *"18 U.S. Code § 2340A - Torture"*. cornell.edu.

12. **Jump up^** PUBLIC LAW 102-256 — MAR. 12, 1992

13. **Jump up^** G. R. Scott, *A History of Torture* (London: Merchant, 1995).

14. **Jump up^** A. Hirsch, *ed.*, *The Book of Torture and Executions* (Toronto: Golden Books, 1944).

15. **Jump up^** Peters, Edward. Torture. New York: Basil Blackwell Inc., 1985.

16. **Jump up^** "Establishment Violence in Philo and Luke: A Study of Non-Conformity to the Torah & Jewish Vigilante Reactions". Seland, Torrey. ISBN 90-04-10252-3, 1995

17. **Jump up^** Catechism of the Catholic Church, 1033, Libreria Editrice Vaticana, ISBN 0-89243-565-8,1994

18.   **Jump up^** J. Franklin, *The Science of Conjecture: Evidence and Probability Before Pascal*. Baltimore: Johns Hopkins University Press, 2001, 26-30.

19.   **Jump up^** Langbein, John H., "Torture and Plea Bargaining" (1978). *Faculty Scholarship Series*. Paper 543. http://digitalcommons.law.yale.edu/fss_papers/543

20.   **Jump   up^** *"Please   visit   our   colleagues   in Bruges!"*. *torturemuseumamsterdam.com*.

21.   **Jump up^** Bately, Janet M. (1986). *The Anglo-Saxon Chronicle: A Collaborative Edition. Vol. 3: MS. A. Cambridge: D.S. Brewer. ISBN 0-85991-103-9*.

22.   **Jump up^** https://www.gutenberg.org/files/5402/5402.txt

23.   **Jump up^** Monter, E. William (1973). "Crime and Punishment in Calvin's Geneva, 1562". Archiv für Reformationsgeschichte 64: 282.

24.   **Jump up^** Parker, T.H.L. (2006). John Calvin: A Biography. Oxford: Lion Hudson plc. ISBN 978-0-7459-5228-4.

25.   **Jump up^** Owen, Robert Dale (1872). The debatable Land Between this World and the Next. New York: G.W. Carleton & Co. p. 69, notes.

26.   **Jump up^** Calvin to William Farel, August 20, 1553, Bonnet, Jules (1820–1892) Letters of John Calvin, Carlisle, Penn: Banner of Truth Trust, 1980, pp. 158–159. ISBN 0-85151-323-9.

27.   **Jump up^** Marshall, John (2006). John Locke, Toleration and Early Enlightenment Culture. Cambridge Studies in Early Modern British History. New York: Cambridge University Press. p. 325. ISBN 0-521-65114-X.

28.   **Jump up^** Levack, Brian P. (1992). Anthropological Studies of Witchcraft, Magic, and Religion. Vol 1 of Articles on Witchcraft, Magic, and Demonology. Garland.

29.   **Jump up^** Jardine, David (1837). A Reading on the Use of Torture in the Criminal Law of England. London: Baldwin and Cradock. pp. 10–12.

30.   **Jump up^** Brizendine, Louann The Female Brain Broadway Books. New York. 2006 pg 36

31.   **Jump up^** See Captives in American Indian Wars

32.   **Jump up^** Napoleon Bonaparte, Letters and Documents of Napoleon, Volume I: The Rise to Power, selected and translated by John Eldred Howard (London: The Cresset Press, 1961), 274.

33.   **Jump up^** History of the Christian Church, Volume IV: Mediaeval Christianity. A.D. 590-1073. Chapter VI. Morals And Religion: Page 80:The Torture by Schaff, Philip (1819-1893)

34.   **Jump up^** Hutchinson's Encyclopaedia: Torture Archived 1 November 2013 at the Wayback Machine.

35.   **Jump up^** Torture - LoveToKnow 1911 Archived 29 May 2013 at the Wayback Machine.

36.   **Jump up^** *"Torture"*. google.com.

37.   **Jump up^** Camille Naish, Death Comes To The Maiden: Sex and Execution 1431-1933 (London: Routledge, 1991), 27.

38. **Jump up^** Henry Charles Lea, *Witchcraft*, pg 236 as quoted in Camille Naish, *Death Comes To The Maiden: Sex and Execution 1431-1933* (London: Routledge, 1991), 28.

39. ^ Jump up to:*a b* H.R. Trevor-Roper, *The European Witch-Craze of The Sixteenth and Seventeenth Centuries and Other Essays,* (New York: Harper and Row, 1969), 120.

40. ^ Jump up to:*a b* H.R. Trevor-Roper, *The European Witch-Craze of The Sixteenth and Seventeenth Centuries and Other Essays,* (New York: Harper and Row, 1969), 121.

41. **Jump up^** Elihu Lauterpacht, C. J. Greenwood *International Law Reports*, Cambridge University Press, 2002 ISBN 0-521-66122-6. ISBN 978-0-521-66122-5 p. 139 section 189

42. ^ Jump up to:*a b c d* Broken Spirits: The Treatment of Traumatized Asylum Seekers, Refugees, War ... edited by Boris Drozðek, John P. Wilson

43. **Jump up^** Tortured confessions: prisons and public recantations in modern Iran - Page 3

44. ^ Jump up to:*a b* "Human Rights Watch - Defending Human Rights Worldwide". *hrw.org.*

45. **Jump up^** "Torture, American style". *Boston.com.*

46. **Jump up^** [Diagnostic and statistical manual of mental disorders: DSM-IV-TR.. 4th ed. Washington, DC: American Psychiatric Association, 2000.]

47. **Jump up^** *Reyes, Hernan (2007). "The Worst Scars are in the Mind: Psychological Torture". The International Review of the Red Cross **89** (867): 591–617.doi:10.1017/s1816383107001300.*

48. **Jump up^** "Executive Order 13491 -- Ensuring Lawful Interrogations". *The White House.*

49. **Jump up^** *Davenport, Christian.* "Helsinki Commission Hearing". *Hearing: "Is It Torture Yet?". US Commission on Security and Cooperation in Europe. Retrieved 21 November 2011.*

50. **Jump up^** "The Death Penalty :Revenge Is the Mother of Invention". *TIME.com. 24 January 1983.*

51. **Jump up^** "Death by a Thousand Cuts at Chinese Arts Centre until 23rd March".*manchestereventsguide.co.uk.*

52. **Jump up^** Dracula - Britannica Concise Archived 30 August 2007 at the Wayback Machine.

53. **Jump up^** Breaking on the wheel - LoveToKnow 1911 Archived 20 July 2013 at the Wayback Machine.

54. **Jump up^** *Merriam-Webster's collegiate dictionary, 10th Edition. Springfield, Mass: Merriam-Webster. 1999. p. 1246. ISBN 0-87779-713-7.*

55. **Jump up^** "Question or Torture". *Retrieved 1 April 2015.*

56. **Jump up^** "Canons of the Fourth Lateran Council, 1215". *canon 3. Retrieved 5 May 2014.*

57. **Jump up^** "SS Innocentius IV – Bulla 'Ad Extirpanda'" *(PDF). 1252. Retrieved 5 May 2014.*

58. **Jump up^** *Ad extirpanda*, quoted at *The Roman Theological Forum*
59. **Jump up^** *Banchoff, Thomas (2007). Democracy and the New Religious Pluralism. p. 147.*
60. **Jump up^** Universal Declaration of Human Rights, United Nations, 10 December 1948
61. **Jump up^** *"What does the law say about torture?". International Committee of the Red Cross.*
62. **Jump up^** ECHR Ireland v. United Kingdom judgment pp. 40,42, ¶ 167 "Although the five techniques, as applied in combination, undoubtedly amounted to inhuman and degrading treatment, although their object was the extraction of confessions, the naming of others and/or information and although they were used systematically, they did not occasion suffering of the particular intensity and cruelty implied by the word torture as so understood."
63. **Jump up^** PDF file of United Nations Committee Against Torture second report on United States of America (CAT/C/48/Add.3/Rev.1) 18 May 2006, Paragraph 14
64. **Jump up^** Optional Protocol to the Convention Against Torture, United Nations, 18 December 2002.
65. **Jump up^** Article 7 of the Rome Statute. Retrieved 11 June 2008.
66. **Jump up^** Article 8 of the Rome Statute. Retrieved 11 June 2008.
67. **Jump up^** Amnesty International, 11 April 2002. *The International Criminal Court — a historic development in the fight for justice.* Retrieved 11 June 2008. Archived 27 April 2015 at the Wayback Machine.
68. **Jump up^** Article 11 of the Rome Statute. Retrieved 11 June 2008.
69. **Jump up^** Articles 12 and 13 of the Rome Statute. Retrieved 11 June 2008.
70. **Jump up^** Articles 17 and 20 of the Rome Statute. Retrieved 11 June 2008.
71. **Jump up^** International Criminal Court. *Office of the Prosecutor.* Retrieved 11 June 2008.
72. **Jump up^** Fourth Geneva Convention, Article 15.
73. **Jump up^** Third Geneva Convention, Article 4
74. **Jump up^** First Geneva Convention, 12 August 1949.
75. **Jump up^** Second Geneva Convention, 12 August 1949.
76. **Jump up^** Third Geneva Convention, 12 August 1949.
77. **Jump up^** Fourth Geneva Convention, 12 August 1949.
78. **Jump up^** Protocol Additional to the Geneva Conventions of 12 August 1949, and relating to the Protection of Victims of International Armed Conflicts (Protocol 1), Diplomatic Conference on the Reaffirmation and Development of International Humanitarian Law applicable in Armed Conflicts, 8 June 1977.
79. **Jump up^** Protocol Additional to the Geneva Conventions of 12 August 1949, and Relating to the Protection of Victims of Non-International Armed Conflicts (Protocol II), Diplomatic Conference on the Reaffirmation and Development of International Humanitarian Law applicable in Armed Conflicts, 8 June 1977.
80. **Jump up^** Standard Minimum Rules for the Treatment of Prisoners, United Nations, Geneva, 1955.

81. **Jump up^** International Covenant on Civil and Political Rights United Nations, 16 December 1966.

82. **Jump up^** European Convention on Human Rights, 4 November 1950(with later protocols).

83. **Jump up^** Ireland v. United Kingdom, 1977. (Case No. 5310/71)

84. **Jump up^** Michael John Garcia (Legislative Attorney American Law Division) U.N. Convention Against Torture (CAT):Overview and Application to Interrogation Techniques CRS Report for Congress 7 November 2005. pp. 13-15

85. **Jump up^** *"About the CPT". coe.int.*

86. **Jump up^** *"Association for the Prevention of Torture". apt.ch.*

87. **Jump up^** *"18 U.S. Code Chapter 113C - TORTURE". cornell.edu.*

88. **Jump up^** *"Decision in Filártiga v. Peña-Irala". Archived from the original on 11 July 2014.*

89. **Jump up^** *Louise Doswald-Beck (March 21, 2011). Human Rights in Times of Conflict and Terrorism. Praeger; 1 edition. p. 220. ISBN 0-1995-7894-X.*

90. **Jump up^** *"Exclusion of evidence obtained through torture". Association for the Prevention of Torture. Retrieved 7 February 2015.*

91. **Jump up^** *"Parliamentary Business>Publications and Records > Commons Publications > Commons Hansard > Daily Hansard -Debate". Parliament.uk. Retrieved 11 July 2009.*

92. **Jump up^** *Gedye, Robin (23 October 2004). "The envoy silenced after telling undiplomatic truths". The Daily Telegraph (London). Retrieved 26 August 2010. Murray fired off a memorandum to the Foreign Office last July suggesting that Britain's intelligence services were wrong to use information gleaned from torture victims*

93. **Jump up^** Torture evidence inadmissible in UK courts, Lords rules,*The Guardian*, 8 December 2005

94. **Jump up^** Torture ruling's international impact by Jon Silverman BBC 8 December 2005

95. **Jump up^** Foreign Office faces probe into 'manipulation', Robert Winnett,*The Sunday Times*, 20 March 2005

96. **Jump up^** Q & A: Torture by Proxy Jane Mayer answers question asked by Amy Davidson The New Yorker on 14 February 2005 Archived 9 July 2014 at the Wayback Machine.

97. **Jump up^** Extraordinary Rendition on Craig Murray's website, 11 July 2005 Archived 28 September 2011 at the Wayback Machine.

98. ^ Jump up to:*ª ᵇ* Q&A: Guantanamo detentions BBC News, 22 January 2009.

99. **Jump up^** Qhatani remains imprisoned at Guantanamo. Woodward, Bob Detainee Tortured, Says U.S. Official Washington Post, 14 January 2009.

100. **Jump up^** *"Court hears arguments over detainee's confession". USA Today. Associated Press. January 13, 2009. Retrieved November 16, 2011.*

101. **Jump up^** *"Guantanamo Judge Rejects Evidence Obtained Through Torture In Jawad Case".yubanet.com.*

102. **Jump up^** *"Guantánamo Judge Throws Out More Evidence Obtained Through Torture In Jawad Case"*. American Civil Liberties Union.

103. **Jump up^** usatoday13Jan2009>

104. ^ Jump up to:[a][b] Weiser, Benjamin,Detainee Acquitted on Most Counts in '98 Bombings New York Times, 17 November 2010

105. ^ Jump up to:[a][b] Rhee, Nissa, Guantánamo detainee's Sentence Renews Debate About Civilian Trials, Christian Science Monitor, 26 January 2011.

106. **Jump up^** *"Consequentialist reasons why torture is wrong"*. BBC. *Archived from the original on 13 December 2007.*

107. ^ Jump up to:[a][b] *Sheehan, Neil (1988). A Bright Shining Lie: John Paul Vann and America in Vietnam(first ed.). Random House. pp. 104, 105.* *ISBN* *978-0-394-48447-1.*

108. **Jump up^** *"Torture and ill-treatment: the arguments: 1. What is torture? What is ill-treatment? What's the difference?"*. Amnesty International. *Archived from the original on 5 December 2007.*

109. **Jump up^** Yasmin Alibhai-Brown: People matter more than holy books Editorial and Opinion (Page 31) in **The Independent** Monday 23 May 2005. Includes commentary on how some Americans have changed their attitudes to torture. Archived 2 October 2014 at theWayback Machine.

110. **Jump up^** Bagaric, Mirko & Clarke Julie:*Not Enough Official Torture in the World? The Circumstances in Which Torture Is Morally Justifiable* University of San Francisco Law Review, Volume 39, Spring 2005, Number 3, pp. 581-616.

111. **Jump up^** "General Says Less Coercion of Captives Yields Better Data" NY Times 7 September 2004

112. **Jump up^** Did torture Work? Washington Post 11 December 2007

113. **Jump up^** David Rose (16 December 2008) "Reckoning" Vanity Fair. Retrieved on 7 June 2009.

114. **Jump up^** Hess, Pamela (19 June 2009) "Gov't delays release of report on interrogations."Associated Press. Retrieved on 20 June 2009. Archived 30 August 2007 at the Wayback Machine.

115. **Jump up^** Seibel, Mark and Strobel, Warren (24 April 2009). "CIA official: No proof harsh techniques stopped terror attacks." McClatchy's. Retrieved on 20 June 2009.

116. **Jump up^** Landay, Jonathan and Strobel, Warren (21 May 2009) "Cheney's speech ignored some inconvenient truths." McClatchy's. Retrieved on 20 June 2009.

117. **Jump up^** *"One third support some torture"*. BBC News. 19 October 2006.

118. **Jump up^** *Ibid*: "*Israel has the largest percentage of those polled endorsing the use of a degree of torture on prisoners, with 43% saying they agreed that some degree of torture should be allowed.*" On the Israeli Supreme Court decision outlawing torture, see Judgment Concerning the Legality of the General Security Service's Interrogation Methods, Supreme Court of Israel, 38 I.L.M. 1471 (1999), and other references at law.harvard.eduArchived 15 April 2015 at the Wayback Machine.

119. **Jump up^** *"New XHTML 1.0 Transitional Compliant Page"*. newspolls.org.

120. **Jump up^** *"Nation: Americans, especially Catholics, approve of torture"*. ncronline.org. *Archived from* the original *on 12 June 2008.*

121. **Jump up^** Pitts, Leonard (7 May 2009). "Commentary: Why do we tolerate torture?" McClatchy's. Retrieved on 19 June 2009.

122. **Jump up^** *Locy, Toni (13 January 2005). "Poll: Most object to extreme interrogation tactics". USA TODAY. Retrieved 20 January 2007. sizable majorities of Americans disagree with tactics*

123. **Jump up^** David Morris and Gary Langer *Poll: Torture Methods Opposed* ABCNEWS.com 27 May 2004 "Americans by nearly 2-to-1 oppose torturing terrorism suspects — but half believe the U.S. government, as a matter of policy, is doing it anyway. And even more think the government is employing physical abuse that falls short of torture in some cases."

124. **Jump up^** Landay, Jonathan (21 April 2009). "Report: Abusive tactics used to seek Iraq-al Qaida link." McClatchy's. Retrieved on 20 June 2009.

125. **Jump up^** (8 September 2006) "Senate report: No Saddam, al-Qaida link." Associated Press. Retrieved on 20 June 2009

126. **Jump up^** Windrem, Robert (13 May 2009). "Cheney's Role Deepens." Daily Beast. Retrieved on 20 June 2009.

127. **Jump up^** Conason, Joe (14 May 2009). "We tortured to justify war." Salon. Retrieved on 20 June 2009. Archived 12 October 2014 at the Wayback Machine.

128. **Jump up^** *"'This Week' Transcript: Former Vice President Dick Cheney". This Week. ABC. 14 February 2010. Retrieved 27 February 2010.*

129. **Jump up^** http://www.timesonline.co.uk, 13 March 2010, "Karl Rove says water torture is justified - and a source of pride" by Giles Whittell

130. **Jump up^** Pentagon investigating link between US military and torture centres in Iraq. Defense Department says 'it will take time' to respond to 15-month investigation by BBC Arabic and the Guardian. By Ewen MacAskill and Mona Mahmood. *The Guardian*, 7 March 2013.

131. **Jump up^** *"A utilitarian argument against torture interrogation of terrorists". springerlink.com.*

132. **Jump up^** *"Educing Information: Interrogation: Science and Art—Foundations for the Future"(PDF). National Defense Intelligence College. December 2006. Retrieved 15 October 2009.*

133. **Jump up^** *"J. Franklin, Evidence gained from torture: wishful thinking, checkability and extreme circumstances" (PDF). Cardozo Journal of International and Comparative Law 17 (2): 281–90. 2009. Retrieved 28 December 2009.*

134. **Jump up^** Report of Conadep (National Commission on the Disappearance of Persons): Prologue- 1984

135. **Jump up^** *"Is torture ever justified?". The Economist. 20 September 2007.*

136. **Jump up^** Bakir, V. Torture, Intelligence and Sousveillance in the War on Terror: Agenda–Building Struggles. Farnham: Ashgate (2013). Available at:http://www.ashgate.com/isbn/9781472402554

137. **Jump up^** Abu Ghraib and the ISA: What's the difference? Archived 20 May 2012 at the Wayback Machine.

138. **Jump up^** Amnesty.org Archived 2 May 2015 at the Wayback Machine.
139. **Jump up^** The National Archives. "Confession of Guy Fawkes." Retrieved 22 April 2007.
140. **Jump up^** Nooria Mehraby. Refugee Women: The Authentic Heroines Archived 30 August 2007 at the Wayback Machine.
141. **Jump up^** *Hoffman, S. J. (2011). "Ending medical complicity in state-sponsored torture" (PDF).The Lancet **378**: 1535–1537. doi:10.1016/S0140-6736(11)60816-7.*
142. **Jump up^** Heger, Heinz. *The Men With the Pink Triangle*. Boston: Alyson Publications, 1980.
143. **Jump up^** *Yamey, Gavin (11 August 2011). "Torture: European Instruments of Torture and Capital Punishment from the Middle Ages to Present". British Medical Journal **323**: 346.doi:10.1136/bmj.323.7308.346.*
144. **Jump up^** Schreiber, Mark. *The Dark Side: Infamous Japanese Crimes and Criminals*. Japan: Kodansha International, 2001. Page 71
145. **Jump up^** Wiehe, Vernon. Sibling Abuse: Hidden Physical, Emotional, and Sexual Trauma. New York: Lexington Books, 1990.
146. **Jump up^** *"What is torture?". IRCT. Retrieved 7 October 2010.*
147. **Jump up^** *"Autopsy reports reveal homicides of detainees in U.S. custody". ACLU.*
148. ^ Jump up to:*a b Nguyen L. (2007). "The question of survival: the death of desire and the weight of life". Am J Psychoanal **67** (1): 53–67. doi:10.1057/palgrave.ajp.3350007.PMID 17510619.*
149. **Jump up^** *"APA Rules on Interrogation Abuse". washingtonpost.com.*
150. ^ Jump up to:*a b c d e f g "Rehabilitation". What is torture?. International Rehabilitation Council for Torture Victims (IRCT). Retrieved 23 March 2011.*
151. **Jump up^** Rehabilitation and Research Centre for Torture Victims: Field Manual on Rehabilitation (2007)

Further reading[edit]

Books

- Campagna, Norbert; Delia, Luigi; Garnot, Benoît (2014), *La Torture, de quels droits? Une pratique de pouvoir (XVIe-XXIe siècle)*, Paris: Éditions Imago. ISBN 978-2-84952-710-8
- *Cobain, Ian (2012). Cruel Britannia: A Secret History of Torture. London: Portobello Books. ISBN 978-1-846-27333-9.*
- *Conroy, John (2001). Unspeakable Acts, Ordinary People: The Dynamics of Torture. California: University of California Press. ISBN 0-520-23039-6.*
- *Levinson, Sanford (2006). Torture: A Collection. Oxford University Press, USA. ISBN 0-19-530646-5.*
- *Maran, Rita (1989). Torture: The Role of Ideology in the French–Algerian War. New York, NY: Praeger.*
- Parry, John T. (2010). *Understanding Torture: Law, Violence, and Political Identity*. Ann Arbor, MI: University of Michigan Press. ISBN 978-0-472-05077-2.

- Reddy, Peter (2005). *Torture: What You Need to Know*, Ginninderra Press, Canberra, Australia. ISBN 1-74027-322-2
- *Rejali, D. M. (1994). Torture & Modernity: Self, Society, and State in Modern Iran. Boulder: Westview Press.*
- *Scarry, Elaine (1985). The body in pain the making and unmaking of the world. Oxford [Oxfordshire]: Oxford University Press. ISBN 0-19-504996-9.*
- *Schmid, Alex P.; Crelinsten, Ronald D. (1994). The politics of pain: torturers and their masters. Boulder, Colo: Westview Press. ISBN 0-8133-2527-7.*
- *Sumanatilake, P. Saliya (2015). Why Do They Torture? A Study On Man's Cruelty. Colombo, Sri Lanka: Stamford Lake (Pvt.) Ltd. ISBN 978-955-658-406-6.*
- *Vreeland, James Raymond (2008). Political Institutions and Human Rights: Why Dictatorships enter into the United Nations Convention Against Torture. International Organization. pp. 62(1):65–101.*
- *Waldron, Jeremy; Colin Dayan (2007). The Story of Cruel and Unusual (Boston Review Books). Cambridge, Mass: MIT Press. ISBN 0-262-04239-8.*

Articles

- *Bromwich, David (2015). "Working the Dark Side". London Review of Books 37 (1): 15– 16.*
- *Danner, Mark (2015). "Our New Politics of Torture". The New York Review of Books 62 (1).*
- *Wantchekon, L. and A. Healy (1999). "The 'Game' of Torture" (PDF). Journal of Conflict Resolution 43 (5): 596–609.*
- *McCoy, Alfred (2014). "How to Read the Senate Report on CIA Torture". History News Network.*

External links

Torture, at the Stanford Encyclopedia of Philosophy.

- Detainee Treatment | Task Force On Detainee Treatment - Report and video - "It Was Torture": Report of the Constitution Project's Task Force on Detainee Treatment, October 7, 2013- The Constitution Project's Task Force on Detainee Treatment
- Medieval Torture - Development, equipment and techniques in Europe

- Chinese Methods of Torture and Execution Photograph collection at University of Victoria, Special Collections
- CPT Database (by the European Committee for the Prevention of Torture and Inhuman or Degrading Treatment or Punishment)
- Freedom from Torture (mostly free) publications and research
- Center for Torture Accountability
- Atlas of Torture - Overview of the situation of torture and ill-treatment around the world (by the Ludwig Boltzmann Institute of Human Rights (BIM) in Vienna, Austria)
- 25 Western Depictions of Crime and Punishment during Qing Dinasty - Collection of 51 images on crime and punishment in late Imperial China.
- The International Rehabilitation Council for Torture Victims (based in Copenhagen, Denmark)

Omarska camp

Omarska

Death camp

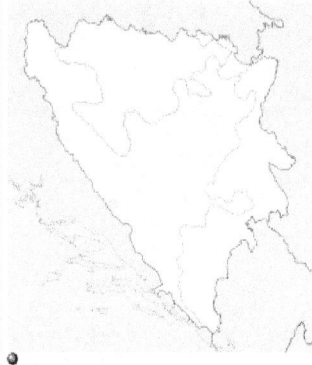

Location of Omarska in Bosnia and Herzegovina

Coordinates	44°51′09″N 16°52′58″ECoordinates: 44°51′09″N 16°52′58″E
Location	Omarska, Prijedor, Bosnia and Herzegovina
Operated by	Bosnian Serb forces
Operational	25 May – 21 August 1992 (2 months, 3 weeks and 6 days)
Inmates	Bosniaks and Croats[1]

Number of inmates	c. 6,000
Killed	700

The **Omarska camp** was a death camp[2] run by Bosnian Serb forces in the mining town of Omarska, near Prijedor in northernBosnia and Herzegovina, set up for Bosniak and Croat men and women during the Prijedor massacre. Functioning in the first months of the Bosnian War in 1992, it was one of 677 alleged detention centers and camps set up throughout Bosnia and Herzegovina during the war.[3] While nominally an "investigation center" or "assembly point" for members of the Bosniak and Croatian population,[4] Human Rights Watch classified Omarska as a concentration camp.[5][6]

The International Criminal Tribunal for the Former Yugoslavia, located in The Hague, has found several individuals guilty of crimes against humanity perpetrated at Omarska. Murder, torture, rape, and abuse of prisoners was common. Around 6,000 Bosniaks and Croats were held in appalling conditions at the camp for about five months in the spring and summer of 1992, including 37 women. Hundreds died of starvation, punishment beatings and ill-treatment.

Overview

Omarska was a predominantly Serb village in northwestern Bosnia, near the town of Prijedor.[7] The camp in the village existed from about 25 May to about 21 August 1992, when the Bosnian Serb military and police unlawfully segregated, detained and confined some of more than 7,000 Bosniaks and Bosnian Croats captured in the ethnic cleansingof Prijedor. Bosnian Serb authorities termed it an "investigation center" and the detainees were accused of alleged paramilitary activities.[8]

By the end of 1992, the war would result in the death or forced departure of most of the Bosniak and Croat population of Prijedor municipality. About 7,000 people went missing from a population of 25,000, and there are 145 mass graves and hundreds of individual graves in the extended region.[9] There is conflicting information about how many people were killed at Omarska. According to survivors, usually about 30 and sometimes as many as 150 men were singled-out and killed in the camp every night.[10] The U.S. State Department and other governments believe that, at a minimum, hundreds of detainees, whose identities are known and unknown, did not survive; many others were killed during the evacuation of the camps in the Prijedor area.[8]

Prijedor massacre

Main article: Prijedor massacre

A declaration on the takeover of Prijedor by Serb forces was prepared by Serbian Democratic Party (SDS) politicians and was repeatedly read out on Radio Prijedor the day after the takeover. Four-hundred Bosnian Serb policemen were assigned to participate in the takeover, the objective of which was to seize the functions of the president of the municipality, the vice-president of the municipality, the director of the post office, the chief of the police, etc. On the night of the 29/30 April 1992, the takeover of power took place. Serb employees of the public security station and reserve police gathered in Cirkin Polje, part of the town of Prijedor. The people there were given the task of taking over power in the municipality and were broadly divided into five groups. Each group of about twenty had a leader and each was ordered to gain control of certain buildings. One group was responsible for the Assembly building, one for the main police building, one for the courts, one for the bank and the last for the post-office.[8] The International Criminal Tribunal for the Former Yugoslavia (ICTY) concluded that the takeover by the Serb politicians was an illegal coup d'état, which was planned and coordinated long in advance with the ultimate aim of creating a pure Serbian municipality. These plans were never hidden and they were implemented in a coordinated action by the Serb police, army and politicians. One of the leading figures was Milomir Stakić, who came to play the dominant role in the political life of the municipality.[8]

Camp

In May 1992, intensive shelling and infantry attacks on Bosniak areas in the municipality caused the Bosniak survivors to flee their homes. The majority of them surrendered or were captured by Serb forces. As the Serb forces rounded up the Bosniak and Croat residents, they forced them to march in columns bound for one or another of the prison camps that the Serb authorities had established in the municipality. On about 25 May 1992, about three weeks after the Serbs took control of the municipal government, and two days after the start of large scale military attacks on Bosniak population centers, Serb forces began taking prisoners to the Omarska camp. During the next several weeks, the Serbs continued to round up Bosniaks and Croats from Kozarac near Prijedor, and other places in the municipality and send them to the camps. Many Bosniak and Croat intellectuals and politicians were sent to Omarska. While virtually all of the prisoners were male, there were also 37 women detained in the camp, who served food and cleaned the walls of the torture rooms, and were repeatedly raped in the canteen; bodies of five of them have been exhumed.[8]

The Omarska mines complex was located about 20 kilometres (12 mi) from Prijedor. The first detainees were taken to the camp at some point between 26 and 30 May. The camp buildings were almost completely full and some of the detainees had to be held in the area between the two main buildings. That area was lit up by specially installed spot-lights after the detainees arrived. Female detainees were held separately in the administrative building. According to the wartime documents of Serb authorities, there were a total of 3,334 persons held in the camp from 27 May to 16 August 1992; 3,197 were Bosniaks, 125 were Croats.[8]

Within the area of the Omarska mining complex that was used for the camp, the camp authorities generally confined the prisoners in three different buildings: the administration building, where interrogations and killings took place; the crammed hangar building; the "white house", where the inmates were tortured; and on a cement courtyard area between the buildings known as the "pista", an L-shaped strip of concrete land in between, also a scene of torture and mass killings. There was another small building, known as the "red house", where prisoners were sometimes taken in order to be summarily executed.[11] With the arrival of the first detainees, permanent guard posts and anti-personnel landmines were set up around the camp. The conditions in the camp were horrible. In the building known as the "white house", the rooms were crowded with 45 people in a room no larger than 20 square metres (220 sq ft). The faces of the detainees were distorted and bloodstained and the walls were covered with blood. From the beginning, the detainees were beaten with fists, rifle butts and wooden and metal sticks. The guards mostly hit the heart and kidneys whenever they decided to beat someone to death. In the "garage", between 150 and 160 people were "packed like sardines" and the heat was unbearable. For the first few days, the detainees were not allowed out and were given only a jerry can of water and some bread. Men would suffocate during the night and their bodies would be taken out the following morning. The room behind the restaurant was known as "Mujo's Room". The dimensions of this room were about 12 m × 15 m (39 ft × 49 ft) and the average number of people detained there was 500, most of whom were Bosniaks. The women in the camp slept in the interrogations rooms, which they would have to clean each day as the rooms were covered in blood and pieces of skin and hair. In the camp one could hear the moaning and wailing of people who were being beaten.[8]

The detainees at Omarska had one meal a day. The food was usually spoiled and the process of getting the food, eating and returning the plate usually lasted around three minutes. Meals were often accompanied by beatings. The toilets were blocked and there was human waste everywhere. British journalist Ed Vulliamy testified that when he visited the camp, the detainees were in very poor physical condition. He witnessed them eating a bowl of soup and some bread and said that he had the impression they had not eaten in a long time; they appeared terrified. According to Vulliamy, the detainees drank water from a river that was polluted with industrial waste and many suffered from constipation or dysentery. No criminal report was ever filed against persons detained in the Omarska camp, nor were the detainees apprised of any concrete charges against them. Apparently, there was no legitimate reason justifying these people's detention.[8]

Murder, torture, rape, and abuse of prisoners was common. Detainees were kept in inhumane conditions and an atmosphere of extreme psychological and physical violence pervaded the camp.[12] The camp guards and frequent visitors who came to the camps used all types of weapons and instruments to beat and otherwise physically abuse the detainees. In particular, Bosnian Muslim and Bosnian Croat political and civic leaders, intellectuals, the wealthy, and other non-Serbs who were considered "extremists" or to have resisted the Bosnian Serbs were especially subjected to beatings and mistreatment which often resulted in death.[13][14]

In addition, the Omarska and Keraterm camps also operated in a manner designed to discriminate and subjugate the non-Serbs by inhumane acts and cruel treatment. These acts included the brutal living conditions imposed on the prisoners. There was a deliberate policy of overcrowding and lack of basic necessities of life, including inadequate food, polluted water, insufficient or non-existent medical care and unhygienic and cramped conditions. The prisoners all suffered serious psychological and physical deterioration and were in a state of constant fear.[15] Inmates were usually killed by shooting, beating or by the cutting of throats; however, in one incident, prisoners were incinerated on a pyre of burning tires. The corpses were then transferred onto trucks by other inmates or using bulldozers. There were instances where prisoners were brought to dig the graves and did not return. The ICTY Trial Chamber in the Stakić case found on the basis of the evidence presented at trial, that "over 100" prisoners were killed at the camp in late July 1992. About 200 people from Hambarine brought to the camp in July 1992 were held in the building known as the "white House". In the early hours of 17 July, gunshots were heard that continued until dawn. Corpses were seen in front of the "white house" and camp guards were seen shooting rounds of ammunition into the bodies. A witness testified that "everyone was given an extra bullet that was shot in their heads". About 180 bodies in total were loaded onto a truck and taken away.[8]

The camp was closed immediately after a visit by foreign journalists in early August. On 6 or 7 August 1992, the detainees at Omarska were divided into groups and transported in buses to different destinations. About 1,500 people were transported on twenty buses.[8]

Death toll

As part of the ethnic cleansing operations, the Omarska, Keraterm, Manjača, and Trnopolje camps helped the Crisis Committee of the Serbian District of Prijedor to reduce the non-Serb population of Prijedor from more than 50,000 in 1992 to little more than 3,000 in 1995, and even fewer subsequently.[2] Precise calculations about the number who actually died in these camps are difficult to make. Newsweek reporter Roy Gutman claimed that US State Department officials, along with representatives of other Western governments, told him that 4,000–5,000 people, the vast majority of them non-Serbs, perished at Omarska.[5] Journalist Bill Berkeley puts the death toll at 2,000.[16] A member of the United Nations (UN) Commission of Experts testified during the trial of Duško Tadić at the ICTY that their number was in the thousands, but she could not be precise, despite the fact that Serbian officials confirmed there were no large scale releases of prisoners sent there. A member of the Crisis Committee, Simo Drljača, who served as chief of police for Prijedor, has stated that there were 6,000 "informative conversations" (meaning interrogations) in Omarska, Keraterm and Trnopolje, and that 1,503 non-Serbs were transferred from those three camps to Manjača, leaving 4,497 unaccounted for according to Human Rights Watch.[5] According to the Association of Camp Detainess of Prijedor 1992, between May and August 1992, around 6,000 prisoners passed through Omarska, 700 of whom were killed.[17]

International reaction

In early August 1992, Vulliamy, Independent Television News (ITN) reporter Penny Marshall, and Channel 4 News reporter Ian Williams gained access to the Omarska camp.[18]Their reporting served as one of the catalysts of a UN effort to investigate war crimes committed in the conflict.[19] The camp was closed less than a month after its exposure caused international uproar.

1997–2000 controversy

Between 1997 and 2000, there was academic and media controversy regarding the events that took place in Omarska and Trnopolje in 1992, due to claims of false reporting and "lies". These allegations, promoted by the state-controlled Radio Television of Serbia (RTS) and the British Living Marxism (LM) paper, prompted the ITN network to accuse the LM of libel; ITN won the case in 2000, effectively forcing the paper to close down.[20][21]

Trials

"We were able to establish that the Omarska camp was one of the most brutal and cruel camps that had been established during the wars in the former Yugoslavia."

Bob Reid, Deputy Chief of Investigations, ICTY Office of the Prosecutor[22]

The Republika Srpska officials responsible for running the camp have since been indicted and found guilty of crimes against humanityand war crimes.

- Commanders of the camp, Miroslav Kvočka, Dragoljub Prcač, Milojica Kos, and Mlađo Radić, and a local taxi driver, Zoran Žigićwere all found guilty of crimes against humanity. Kvočka, Prcač, Kos and Radić were sentenced to five, six, seven and 20 years respectively; Žigić was given the longest term of 25 years.[23]
- Željko Mejakić was found guilty of crimes against humanity (murder, imprisonment, torture, sexual violence, persecution, and other inhumane acts). He was the *de facto* commander of Omarska and perpetrated one instance of mistreatment. It was found that

he was part of a joint criminal enterprise with the intent of promoting mistreatment and persecution of detainees in the camp. He was sentenced to 21 years of imprisonment.[24]

- Momčilo Gruban was found guilty of crimes against humanity (murder, imprisonment, torture, sexual violence, persecution, and other inhumane acts). He had command responsibility for crimes committed at the camp and acted as part of a joint criminal enterprise. He was sentenced to 11 years imprisonment.[24]

- Duško Knežević was found guilty of crimes against humanity (murder, torture, sexual violence, persecution, and other inhumane acts). He was found to have been directly involved in the crimes carried out in the Omarska and Keraterm camps. He was also found guilty under the theory of joint criminal enterprise for furthering the Omarska and Keraterm camps' systems of mistreatment and persecution of detainees. He was sentenced to 31 years imprisonment.[24]

On 26 February 2007, the International Court of Justice (ICJ) presented its judgment in the Bosnian Genocide Case, in which it had examined atrocities committed in detention camps, including Omarska, in relation to Article II (b) of the Genocide Convention. The Court stated in its judgment:

Having carefully examined the evidence presented before it, and taken note of that presented to the ICTY, the Court considers that it has been established by fully conclusive evidence that members of the protected group were systematically victims of massive mistreatment, beatings, rape and torture causing serious bodily and mental harm during the conflict and, in particular, in the detention camps. The requirements of the material element, as defined by Article II *(b)* of the Convention are thus fulfilled. The Court finds, however, on the basis of evidence before it, that it has not been conclusively established that those atrocities, although they too may amount to war crimes and crimes against humanity, were committed with the specific intent (*dolus specialis*) to destroy the protected group, in whole or in part, required for a finding that genocide has been perpetrated.[25]

Exhumations

Ed Vulliamy speaking at the 2006 Omarska camp commemoration

In 2004, a mass grave located a few hundred meters from the Omarska site was unearthed containing the remains of 456 persons from the camp.[26] "There is no doubt whatsoever that there are hundreds of bodies as yet unfound within the mine of Omarska and its vicinity" said Amor Mašović, president of the Bosnian government's Commission for Tracing Missing Persons.[27][28] The International Commission on Missing Persons (ICMP) has been active in advocating the exhumation and identification of their bodies from mass graves around the area; with their help, a number of victims have been identified through DNA testing.[29]

Memorial controversy

The Mittal Steel company purchased the Omarska mining complex and planned to resume extraction of iron ore from the site.[30] Mittal Steel announced in Banja Luka on 1 December 2005 that the company would build and finance a memorial in the 'White House' but the project was later abandoned. Many Bosnian Serbs believe there should not be a memorial, while many Bosniaks believe that construction should be postponed until all the victims are found and only if the entire mine—which is in use—be allocated for the memorial site.[31]

By the time of the 20th anniversary of the camp's closure proposals for a physical memorial to the camp's existence had made no progress. ArcelorMittal said that it was prepared to meet the former inmates' demands but the local authorities were ultimately responsible for granting permission. The Republika Srpska authorities considered that allowing camp survivors free access to the site and the construction of a memorial as originally agreed by ArcelorMittal would undermine reconciliation. "Prijedor 92" president Mirsad Duratović, stated that the campaign for a memorial would continue.[32]

In July 2012, ahead of the start of the 2012 London Olympic Games, survivors of the camp laid claim to the ArcelorMittal Orbit tower, the tallest structure in Britain, located in the Olympic Park beside the Olympic stadium, as the 'Omarska Memorial in Exile'. The survivors allege that the Orbit is "tragically intertwined with the history of war crimes in Bosnia, as the bones of victims are mixed in with the iron ore". ArcelorMittal denied that material from Omarska had been used in the Orbit's construction. The company said that sensitive issues relating to the mine could not be addressed by ArcelorMittal on its own. Campaigners urged ArcelorMittal as the world's largest steel producer to use its considerable influence to oppose the local politics of denial and play an active role in healing fractured communities that have made the company's success possible. Susan Schuppli of the Centre for Research Architecture at Goldsmiths' College in London, observed that ArcelorMittal insistence on "not taking sides" in an area where persecution and injustice continued was not neutrality but taking a political position by default.

See also

- Bosnian Genocide
- Serbian war crimes in the Yugoslav Wars
- Dretelj camp
- Gabela camp
- Heliodrom camp
- Uzamnica camp
- Vilina Vlas
- Vojno camp

References

Notes

Footnotes

1. **Jump up^** *Ed Vuliamy (10 September 2004). "Return to Omarska". The Guardian. Retrieved 17 November 2012.*
2. ^ Jump up to:[a b] *"Final report of the United Nations Commission of Experts established pursuant to security council resolution 780 (1992)". United Nations – Security Council. 28 December 1994.*
3. **Jump up^** *"Prison camps". Final Report of the Commission of Experts. Established Pursuant to Security Council Resolution 780. United Nations. 27 May 1994.*
4. **Jump up^** *Simons, Marlise (3 November 2001). "5 Bosnian Serbs Guilty of War Crimes at Infamous Camp". The New York Times.*
5. ^ Jump up to:[a b c] *"The Unindicted: Reaping the Rewards of "Ethnic Cleansing" in Prijedor". Human Rights Watch. 1 January 1997.*
6. **Jump up^** *Argentine Forensic Anthropology Team. "A mission to assist with field and laboratory work for the International Criminal Tribunal to the former Yugoslavia in its investigation into human rights violations in Bosnia." (PDF).*
7. **Jump up^** *Helsinki Watch. War Crimes in Bosnia-Hercegovina 2. New York: Human Rights Watch. p. 87. ISBN 1-56432-097-9.*
8. ^ Jump up to:[a b c d e f g h i j] *"ICTY: Milomir Stakić judgement" (PDF).*
9. **Jump up^** *Vulliamy, Ed (1 September 2004). "Fingers stuck up at the Serbs". Salon.*
10. **Jump up^** *Vulliamy, Ed (1 September 2004). "'We can't forget'". The Guardian.*
11. **Jump up^** *"ICTY: Miroslav Kvočka, Mlado Radić, Zoran Žigić and Dragoljub Prcać judgement"(PDF).*
12. **Jump up^** *May, Larry (2007). War Crimes and Just War. Cambridge University Press. p. 237. ISBN 0-521-87114-X.*
13. **Jump up^** *"Mejakić Željko and others, First Instance Verdict" (PDF). Court of Bosnia and Herzegovina. 30 May 2008.*

14. **Jump up^** _"Mejakić Željko and others, Second Instance Verdict"_ (PDF). Court of Bosnia and Herzegovina. 16 February 2009.

15. **Jump up^** _"Prosecutor v. Predrag Banović, Sentencing Judgment"_ (PDF). International Criminal Tribunal for the former Yugoslavia. 28 October 2003.

16. **Jump up^** Bill Berkeley (13 January 2002). _"Conspiring Against Humanity"_. The New York Times. Retrieved 17 November 2012.

17. **Jump up^** _"Victims of Bosnia's Omarska Jail Camp Remembered"_. Balkan Insight. 6 August 2016. Retrieved 19 February 2016. "According to our data, between May and August 1992, around 6,000 prisoners went through Omarska, 700 of whom were killed either inside the gates or at various execution grounds," said Mirsad Duratovic, president of the Association of Camp Detainess of Prijedor 1992.

18. **Jump up^** Vulliamy, Ed (7 August 1992). _"Shame of camp Omarska"_. The Guardian.

19. **Jump up^** Vulliamy, Ed (8 June 1996). _"'Some were thin, others skeletal'"_. The Guardian.

20. **Jump up^** Campbell, David (March 2002). _"Atrocity, memory, photography: imaging the concentration camps of Bosnia – the case of ITN versus Living Marxism, Part 1"_ (PDF).Journal of Human Rights _1_ (1): 1–33. doi:_10.1080/14754830110111544_.

21. **Jump up^** Campbell, David (June 2002). _"Atrocity, memory, photography: imaging the concentration camps of Bosnia – the case of ITN versus Living Marxism, Part 2"_ (PDF). Journal of Human Rights _1_ (2): 143–172. doi:_10.1080/14754830210125656_.

22. **Jump up^** _"Bridging the Gap in Prijedor, Bosnia and Herzegovina"_. International Criminal Tribunal for the former Yugoslavia.

23. **Jump up^** Osborn, Andrew (3 November 2001). _"Five Serbs guilty of Omarska camp atrocities"_.The Guardian.

24. ^ Jump up to:[a][b][c] _"Eighth Report in the Željko Mejakic et al. Case"_ (PDF). Organization for Security and Co-operation in Europe Mission to Bosnia and Herzegovina. June 2008.

25. **Jump up^** _"The Application of the Convention on the Prevention and Punishment of the Crime of Genocide (Bosnia and Herzegovina v. Serbia and Montenegro), case 91"_ (PDF). International Court of Justice. 26 February 2007. p. 119.

26. **Jump up^** Keulemans, Chris (26 June 2007). _"Omarska – Fifteen Years On"_. Bosnian Institute.

27. **Jump up^** Vulliamy, Ed (2 December 2004). _"New battle breaks out over Serb death camp"_. The Guardian.

28. **Jump up^** Vulliamy, Ed (2 December 2004). _"In pursuit of reconciliation"_. Salon.

29. **Jump up^** Boyle, Katherine (12 January 2007). _"Bosnia: A House Divided"_. Institute for War & Peace Reporting.

30. **Jump up^** Vulliamy, Ed (3 December 2004). _"Sale of Omarska"_. Bosnian Institute.

31. **Jump up^** Hawton, Nick (20 February 2006). _"Bosnia war memorial plan halted"_. BBC.

32.   **Jump up^** *Sito-Sucic, Daria (6 August 2012). "Bosnia camp survivors protest for memorial at ArcelorMittal mine". Reuters UK.*
33.   **Jump up^** *"ArcelorMittal's Olympics showpiece in a row". Zee News. 3 July 2012.*

External links[edit]

- Concentration Camps - The Horrors Of A Camp Called Omarska And The Serb Strategy, *PBS*
- The International Tribunal for the former Yugoslavia charges 21 Serbs with atrocities committed inside and outside the Omarska death camp, *ICTY*, 13 February 1995
- Who cares as judgement falls on Serb hell camp?, *The Guardian*, 1996
- Omarska Camp, Bosnia – Broken Promises of "Never Again" by Kelly D. Askin, "Human Rights", published by American Bar Association
- New battle breaks out over Serb death camp, *The Guardian*, 2 December 2004
- 'We can't forget', *The Guardian*, 1 September 2004
- Ex-foes make peace at Omarska, BBC, 21 November 2005

Sušica camp

The **Sušica camp** was a detention camp set up by Serb forces for Bosniaks and other non-Serbs in the Vlasenica municipality in eastern Bosnia and Herzegovina.[1]

Contents

The camp

The detention camp comprised two main buildings and a small house. The detainees were housed in a hangar which measured approximately 30 by 50 meters. Between late May and October 1992, as many as 8,000 Bosniak civilians and other non-Serbs from Vlasenica and the surrounding villages were successively detained in the hangar at Sušica camp. The number of detainees in the hangar at any one time was usually between 300 and 500. The building was severely overcrowded and living conditions were deplorable.[1]

Men, women and children were detained at the camp, sometimes entire families. Women and children as young as eight years old were usually detained for short periods of time and then forcibly transferred to nearby Muslim areas. The men were held in the camp until its closure in late September 1992, and were then transferred to the larger Batković concentration camp near the town of Bijeljina. Women of all ages were raped or sexually assaulted during their time in the camp by camp guards or other men who were allowed to enter the camp.[1]

Male detainees of the camp suffered a similar fate as the women. They were bullied, tortured and murdered.[1] According to Pero Popovic, a former guard at the camp, they were generally lined up against an electricity pylon just outside the barracks and shot.[2] Detainees at Sušica performed forced labour, sometimes at the front lines. Some detainees were killed by camp guards or died from mistreatment. A massacre was committed during the night of 30 September 1992, when the remaining 140 to 150 detainees at Sušica camp were driven out of the camp with buses and executed.[3]

War crime verdict

Dragan Nikolić, the commander of the camp, plead guilty to crimes against humanity and was sentenced to 20 years imprisonment.[1] Predrag Bastah and Goran Višković were sentenced to 22 years and 18 years of imprisonment, respectively, for their involvement at the Sušica camp.[4]

See also

- Bosnian Genocide

- [Dretelj camp](#)
- [Gabela camp](#)
- [Heliodrom camp](#)
- [Keraterm camp](#)
- [Manjača camp](#)
- [Omarska camp](#)
- [Trnopolje camp](#)
- [Uzamnica camp](#)
- [Vilina Vlas](#)

References[edit]

1. ^ Jump up to:*a* *b* *c* *d* *e* *"Dragan Nikolić Case Information Sheet"* (PDF). *International Criminal Tribunal for the former Yugoslavia.*
2. **Jump up^** *Cohen, Roger (2 August 1994). "Bosnian Camp Survivors Describe Random Death". New York Times.*
3. **Jump up^** *"Prosecutor v. Momcilo Krajisnik judgement"* (PDF). *International Criminal Tribunal for the Former Yugoslavia. 17 March 2009.*
4. **Jump up^** *"Bastah Predrag and Others". The Court of Bosnia and Herzegovina.*

Instances of Torture

Samir Avdic, Nedzad Hasic, Ahmo Harbas and Behrudin Husic were severely tortured to sign bogus confessions about the crimes against Serb civilians around Srebrenica. Here is an update of this case from Dnevni Avaz:

Damir Alagic, lawyer representing Samir Avdic who is currently in prison in Foca, stated that his client was forced into signing 102-page long statement about the alleged crimes of Bosniaks against the Bosnian Serb population around Srebrenica.

This bogus statement was drafted by the Serbian Radical Party "Dr. Vojislav Seselj" and "mechanically" signed.

"This shameful policy of equalization of crimes in the Srebrenica area is led by the Greater-Serbian political activists," said Alagic.

He added that in the presense of the lawyer Muhamed Susic, Avdic stated in front of the court in Banja Luka that Serbs who tortured him promised to let him go from prison in a matter of two months if he signs bogus statement implicating a number of Bosniaks in alleged crimes against Serbs in the Srebrenica region.

"Therefore, we consider this statement irrelevant because it was forced, and we know well the degree of psychological abuse our client went through after being severely tortured by Serb authorities who arrested him in 1996."

The defence has a witness who confirms the alibi that the defendant Samir Avdic was not in the place where alleged murder too place. He was in a different location, said Susic.

Zulfo Salihovic, president of the organization of veterans (demobilized soldiers) who served in the Army of Republic of Bosnia-Herzegovina, also believes that Samir Avdic was forced to sign the statement.

"I know Saban Avdic who was not even a soldier, but a local Bosniak miller. As a civilians, he did not survive the fall of Srebrenica, but Serbs accused him of war crimes.

Hakija Meholjic, Zulfo Tursunovic and Smajo Mandza had been questioned by Serb authorities, but there was no evidence to start the proceedings against them," said Salihovic.

Dnevni Avaz

TORTURE OF BOSNIAKS IN SANJAK (SERBIA AND MONTENEGRO)

Newly updated @ November 17, 2008.

BREAKING THE SILENCE: According to the Sanjak Committee for Protection of Human Rights and Freedoms, "Although the authorities of Serbia, Montenegro and the Federal Republic of Yugoslavia were trying to prove that there hasn't been any violations of human rights and freedom of Bosniaks [in Sanjak]... the facts were telling the opposite story."

Disclaimer: The following material contains photos of Bosniaks Muslims tortured by the Serbian Police. Some people may find this material disturbing. All photos are courtesy of the SanjakCommittee for Protection of Human Rights and Freedoms.

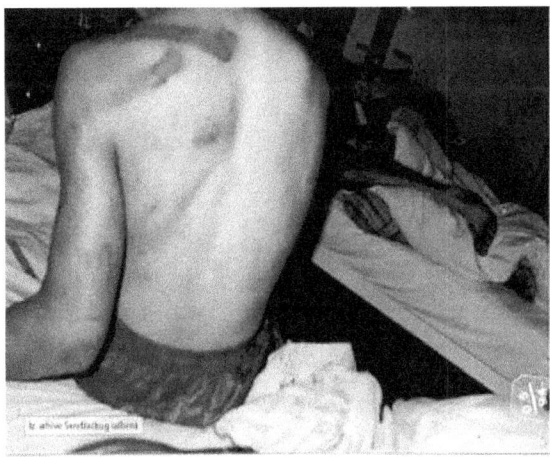

Sanjak (Bosnian: *Sandžak*) is a region, divided between Serbia and Montenegro, mainly populated by Bosniaks Muslims. During 1990s, it was a place of brutal killings, torture and ethnic cleansing of the Bosniak population perpetrated by the oppressive Serbian regime. Hundreds of Bosniak Muslim villages in Sanjak were ethnically cleansed, looted and burned to the ground. Many people were killed and many went missing. Serbian regime kept the area under tight military control and intense media blockade.

For example, until 1992 Bosniaks had lived
in Sjeverin, Kukurovici, Milanovici,Zaostro, Socica, Zivinac, Voskovina,Jelovik, Batkovic
i, Medjurecje, Radnje,Dragovici and then, they disappeared.

In the spring and summer of 2006, a team of human rights activists from
theSandzak Committee for Protection of Human Rights and Freedoms visited ethnically
cleansed Bosniak Muslim villages
in Priboj municipality: Kukorovići, Valovlje, Lisičine, Voskovina, and Sjeverin. By that
time, only few residents returned to their pre-war homes. These villages were
completely destroyed and burned to the ground, while Bosniak population was forced to
flee from their homes - with many residents killed or missing.

The Sanjak Committee for Defence of
Human Rights and Freedoms publisheda book "Svedocenja iz Sandzaka" (*Testimonies
from Sandzak*), documenting numerous victims' testimonies and human rights abuses
in the area. The book is currently available in Bosnian language **here**(unfortunately,
English version is still not available). However, here are some excerpts from two reports
published in English language by the human rights committee.

Report I: Excerpts from "*an Outline of the Status of Human Rights and Freedoms in Sandzak 1991-2006*," published by the Sanjak Committee for Protection of Human Rights and Freedoms follows:

In the spring and summer of 1992, towns and suburbs in Sandzak were in a frightening, complete tanks-cannon surrounding by different units of the Army of Yugoslavia. Some parties, like radicals, were threatening and calling on clearing from Bosniaks bordering parts of Serbia and Montenegro towards Bosnia.

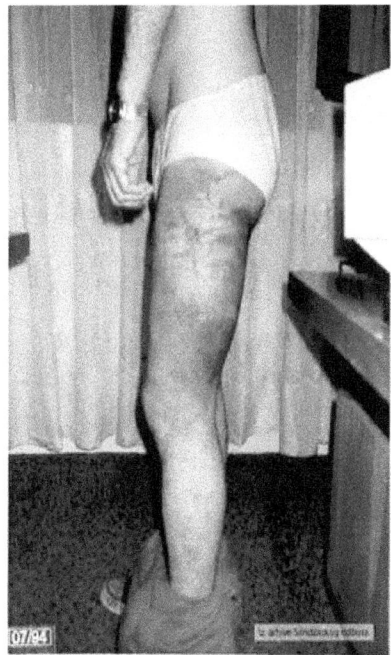 Threatening behaviour by the Army, demonstration of force, everyday low flights of military aviation over the towns and villages, unrestrained paramilitary formations going to Bosnia through Sandzak, many incidents, legal insecurity and an ultimate uncertainties produced great fear and anxiety of repeating «Bosnian scenario», what influenced mass emigrations of Bosniaks towards West European countries. In the spring and summer of 1992, the authorities were literally catching refugees for Bosnia handing them over Serbian authority's mercy in Bosnia. The same situation was going on in Serbia after fall of Srebrenica (during the Srebrenicagenocide) in the summer of 1995.

Bosniak population in Sandzak, apart from all the troubles and problems that was exposed to, warmly accepted refugees staying for longer or shorter time in Sandzak towns. Mass fires and continual bomb attacks particularly on Bosniaks` houses and shops in Pljevlja, as well as attacking Bosniaks in the villages of Bukovica, in

the time of tyrannical regime of chetnic duke and federal
representativeMilika Ceka Dacevic, will start new wave of emigrations.

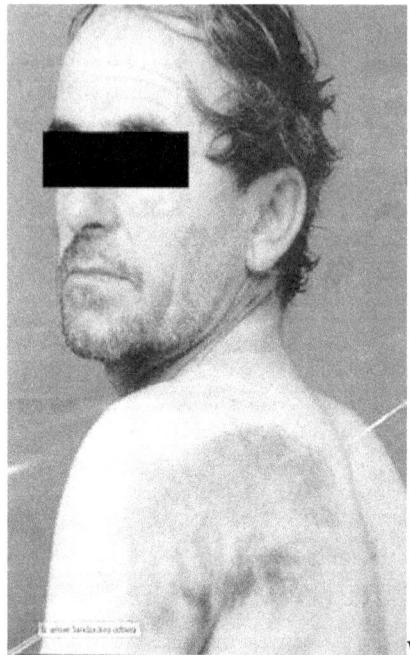

Within an overall frightening
of Bosniaks inSandzak there were abductions of Bosniaks(Mioca near Sjeverin -
22th October 1992- 17 people; Bukovica – 16th February – 11 people; 27th February
1993 Strpci – 19 people), marathon court-political processes in Sandzak during 1994
(Trials in NoviPazar and Bijelo Polje) against a part of leaders and members
of SDA Sandzak, after mass arrests in the summer of 1993 and winter 1994. with an
accusation that they intended to create «the state Sandzak» by force, had aim, besides a
non sense indictment they wanted to imperil SFRY, was followed by great media
campaign to eliminate and marginalize this mainBosniak political party and frighten
and disorientate Bosniaks.

Arrested Bosniaks experienced big tortures in order to admit nonexistent crimes. Along
with these political processes during 1994, there were continued mass police actions of
arresting and beating Bosniaks looking for weapons, although it had been known the
reality and weakness of the state organs to provide them security made Bosniaks to arm
themselves for protection of lives and human dignity. Tens of thousands of people
passed through police «treatment», especially
in Sjenica, Tutin and Novi Pazar, Prijepolje,Rozaje... There were also many cases of

mistreating and hurting Bosniaks performing military service in the units of Yugoslav Army. Attacks involved even mosques, Islamic monuments and cemeteries.

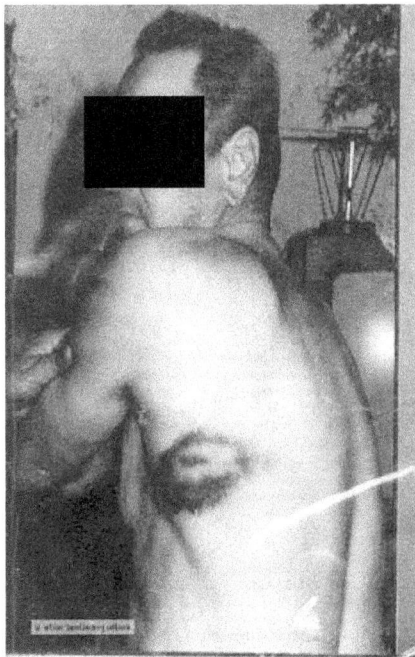

From media propaganda arsenal, particularly during 1992, old pejoratives «national nicknames» were brought back into the use. Bosniaks were characterized again odious «Turkish» enemies.

CallingBosniaks «Turks» with the majority is not a consequence of lack of information, but a rooted prejudice and a totally concrete attitude. Sandzak and Bosniaks in it, during the time of total uncertainties and closeness and echo of Bosnian battlefields, had been exposed to various troubles and temptations... One could get an impression the authorities tried to provoke an armed protest by Bosniaks in order to get demanded justification to stop it with all available means and in that way the number of Bosniaks in this region, by various forms of scare tactics and torture, reduce to the least possible quantity. Media reports from Sandzak mainly included news aimed at creating and/or confirming an an already popular stereotypes of Bosniaks, picturing them as extremists and fanatics.

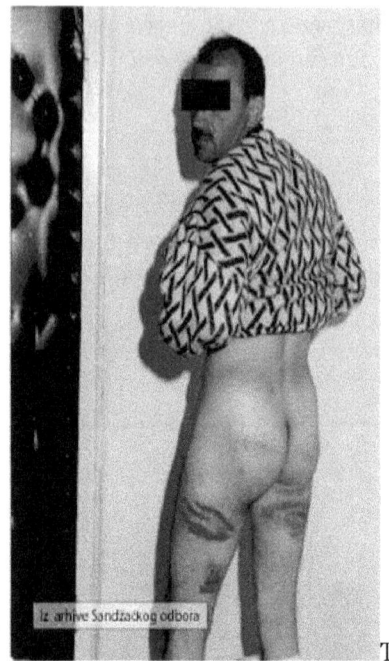

Iz arhive Sandžačkog odbora

There is a persistent change of
terms Sandzakwith the term Raska oblast (Raska field). NoviPazar is called
« Turkicized Raska». Asynchronical media satanization of this region aimed at showing
that Bosniaks in this region are «fundamentalists», «Islamic extremists», they support
so called «green transfersal» ("Zelena Transferzala = Green Bridgehead), they are
preparing for the war, they have 15.000 armed people, divided into brigades and
battalions. The leading media were: Vecernjenovosti», «Politika ekspres», «Politika»
and «Pobjeda». Paralel with breaking out the war in Bosnia, an aggressive campaign
againstBosniaks was continued, especially after permanently repeated news that in
«former Bosnia and Herzegovina», «Alija's jamahiria» the main warriors are
just Sandzak people, that Bosnia wants to join Sandzak, that «Sword of Islam is
threatening Raska», that there is a systematic work on planned uniting of Muslims,
which variant is so called half-moon, i.e. the road Sarajevo-Novi Pazar-Pristina-Skopje-
Sofija-Ankara.

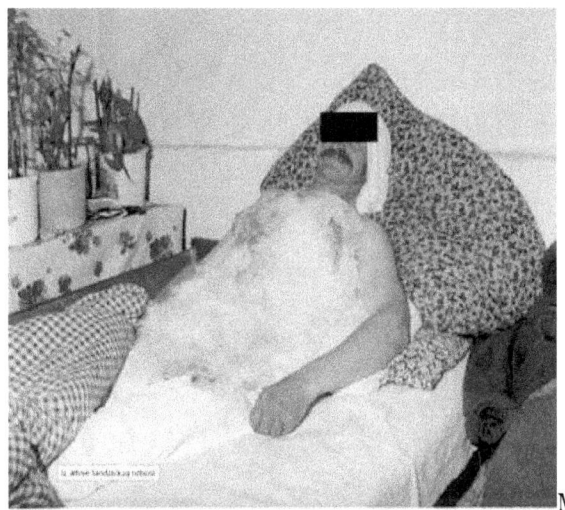

Mass illusion of armed «fanatics» and «fundamentalists» from Sandzak became an obsession not only of media but politicians, as well. By intruding one-sided information, by theories on a supposed sucidal nature ofBosniaks and by permanent, racial announcements that it is impossible to live together with Bosniaks in Bosnia any longer, media attacks were becoming more and more unscrupulous, with an aim to representBosniaks in Sandzak as collective conspirators and the world danger.

....While the Hague [ICTY] brought indictments for crimes being committed in Croatia, Bosnia, in Kosovo and Vojvodina, Sandzak was completely marginalized. Carla del Ponte in an interview for Podgorica «Monitor» stressed that all the crimes can`t be treated in Hague, that national courts must deal with the problem of war crimes, and that «case Strpci» must also be resolved at the courts of Serbia and Montenegro. Many crimes have simply been forgotten, although they must be the subject of interest of the state and courts.

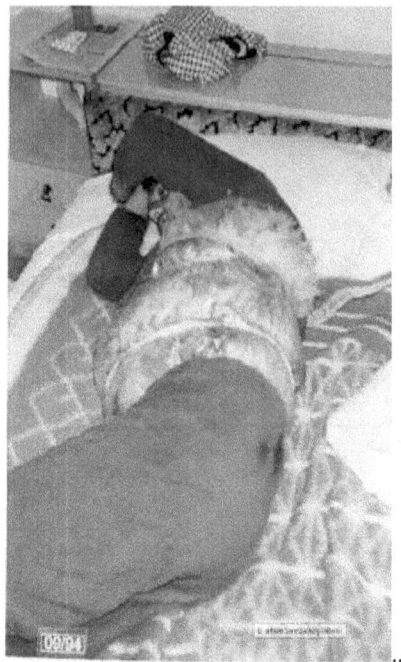....The fact is that changes in Serbia, since 2000 are happening, but very slowly. They could be seen in bigger areas more than in the towns like Novi Pazar, Tutin or Sjenica. Weshouldn`t even talk about remote villages ofSandzak. The reasons for that are deep, pressured by the past, but also by the present. Experience we had with Serbia's passing of Laws on National Minorities, made on the federal level, being followed by media pomp, showed indications that those laws were passed mostly under the International pressure, and less with a sincere wish of the state authorities to improve human rights and provide protection and affirmation of the minority communites.

Report II: **"General situation in Sanjak" (sections: *"The attitude of the authorities towards violation of human rights and freedoms"* and *"Protection of the victims' rights"*), published by the theSanjak Committee for Protection of Human Rights and Freedoms follows:**

Sandzak Committee is worried for the permanent unreadiness of the state organs to sanction the crimes being done between 1992 and 2000. at the territory of Serbia and upon its residents (case Sjeverin, Strpci, Kukurovici, 1, burning, robberies, murders, proscriptions of Bosniak population from Priboj commune, various forms of institutional discrimination, court-political processes, brutal police actions, etc.

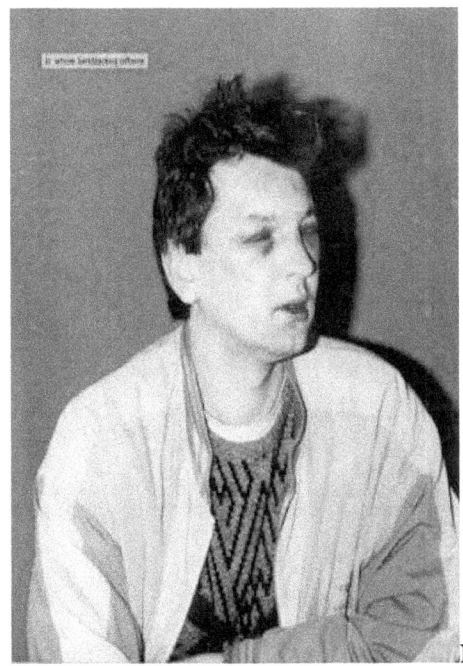

Numerous criminal charges by the victims, according to the evidence of SandzakCommittee, for Court disorganization, prolonging, synchronical obstructions have already expired. Many people, even 13 years later can't achieve their rights. In that context, we will remind, just for an illustration, of a marathon court process of trial to the group of 24 Bosniaks in Novi Pazar being started in 1993., as well as of the case „Djerlek", being known to domestic NGOs for human rights and International organizations, that haven't been closed even 10 years later and have been expired. Also, in the court procedures fromcases where criminal charges have been brought by Sandzak Committee (May-June 2001. and February 2002.) against the Serbianpolicemen, second instance sentences haven't still been brought.

...Criminal charge before the District Court inNovi Pazar, started in May 2003 against 24 Bosniaks hasn't still been resolved. More than 13 years the rights of the accused are partially reduced. They are under heavy accusation, without visible signs of possible end. The Committee believes this issue has conditions to be shifted to the competence of International Court, since the domestic courts are not capable of solving the problem. However, for the lack of budget to pay the layers of the accused, the activity of the Committee is focused on monitoring this process before the domestic courts.

Families from Priboj commune which houses were burnt 1992.-1997 in their address to theSandzak Committee stress chronic impossibility of return to their properties, since some houses were destroyed some weren't, for the lack of budget and absence of care of the state, and reconstructing them. They are persistant in the demand formSandzak Committee to start the criminal charge against the state in the aim of compensation for the damages being done to them. For the financial problems SandzakCommittee wasn't able to engage attorneys in this case, but it applied with other NGOs in Belgrade with which it has a fruitful, long cooperation, which are ready to help legally to these people in those requests.

....By the end of May the representatives of Sandzak Committee visited Priboj villages being damaged during the nineties, whenBosniaks were being expelling from their own homes, killed and frightened. What is worrying is that even 13 years after this crime, the statehadn't done anything to help the families of the killed, as well as to the displaced to return to their homes.

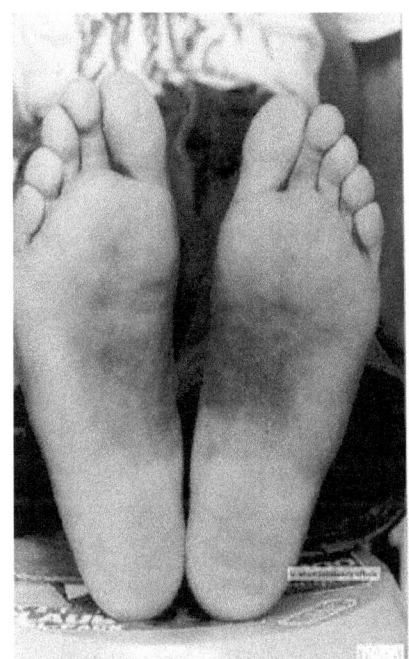

Until 1992. Bosniaks have lived in Sjeverin, Kukurovici, Milanovici, Zaostro, Socica, Zivinac, Voskovina, jelovik, Batkovici, Medjurecje, Radnje, Dragovici and then, they disapeared. The ethnic cleansing started in the villages with mainly Bosniak population.Priboj is still being forgotten, first of all, by the state organs and institutions. During the last 13 years the state hasn't done anything to help the damaged. As Hamed Pecikoza said they contacted the Government and many other organs of the local power four times. No answer. Many NGOs addressed the competent representatives of authorities, but there was no progress. The relation of the local administration to what was happening with Bosniaks in Priboj is still a special story. As Pecikoza said addressing local authorites was waste of time, since thehave always sent them somewhere else.

The mentioned Priboj villages where Bosniaks used to live seem forget 13 years later. Devastation much worse than at the first days after deportion. There was enough time for all the furniture to be stolen from homes. Many houses and annexes that hadn`t been destroyed by the war remained even without windows, doors, roofs...Even wall wooden covers were taken away, floors.

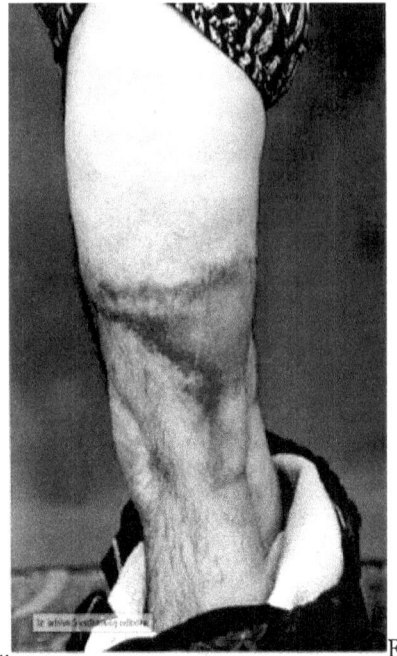

.... Everything was, in the full sense of the word, devastated. During the nineties the Army of FRY was staying in the houses and traces are pretty visible. There is no house that hasn't been almost destroyed and without traces of soldiers. That way the houses were even more damaged. There were written different names on the walls, the names of the cities, oaths and many outrageous messages based on insults on national basis. There is no correct information how many families left their homes. The exile was particularly massive in the villages on the border with Bosnia. All the homes of exiled Bosniaks were robbed and destroyed. People were leaving with only one bag in their hands. The sticks depended on the mercy of the neighbours. Hamid Pecikoza gave a good example when we visited him. Hilmo Alivodic`s house was saved thanks to the neighbour Dobrisav Radovic. "Different gangs were coming to rob the house but Radovic offered resistance. You can see what means to have a nice neighbour. But this case is the only one. If only there had been more such people, said Pecikoza.

The representatives of Sandzak Committee visted: Sjeverin, Strmac, Milanoviće, Voskovina, Batkovići and some others. We found an older couple who returned. There is no return since there is no money for reconstructing the houses. The necessary budget exceeds capacities of the Municipality of Priboj. Only in Kukurovici, as Pecikoza said, some houses had been renewed thanks to donations. The exiled Bosnjaks have been able to see their properties since 2000. But there are no conditions for living there, and fear hasn't been uprooted yet. Nobody was interogatedfor burning the houses, for murders and ethnic cleansing there.

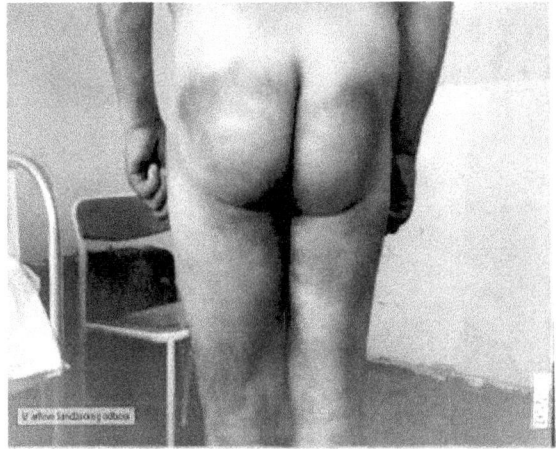

...In villages Krajcinovici and Zabrnjice (Priboj commune) a decision to close schools, caused 18 returnee students to walk 10 kilometers to the nearest school, and forced returnee Bosniak families to leave these villages altogether.

James Lion from the International Crisis Group, presenting the report about „Serbian Sandzak", in Priboj on 7th July 2005. said:

"We described the situation in the 6 towns of Sandzak belonging to Serbia and called the report 'Serbian Sandzak' so that International Community could realise waht is going on here and what kinds of problems are here. Our wish and aim is that region not to be seen as an area of potential interethnic conflicts. The problem here is economy, since there is an economic and social disaster here. In the near future I cannot see any hope for this area, by the Government from Belgrade or by the International Community. Another problem is recent past. WE must know the truth about Sandzak.

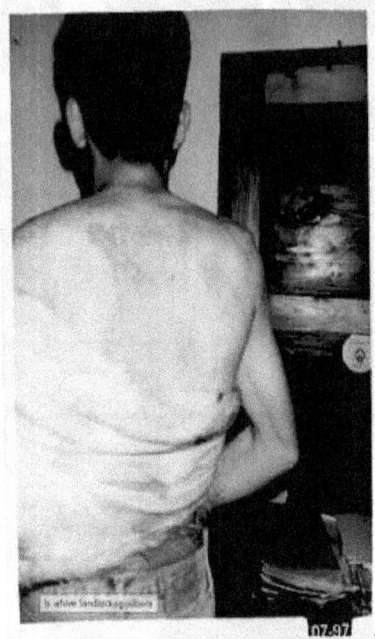

I have been in Sandzak for almost five years. Crimes had been done here. In our report we wrote that in the municipality of Priboj about 20 villages were 'ethnically cleansed' of Bosniaks. During that action 185 houses were burnt or destroyed and 23 Bosnjaks were killed. We especially processed the cases of murders of three Bosniaks during attacks on the village Kukurovici, abduction of 17 Bosniaks from Sjeverin, who were killed in Visegrad, abduction of 20 Bosniaks in Strpce, actions of ethnic cleansing in the region of Bukovica in the commune of Pljevlja, massive dismissals of Bosniaks from work, especially in Priboj. Simply, we must face these crimes."

JUDGE, CAPTAIN DRAGAN COMMITTED TORTURE & RAPE

PHOTO: Captain Dragan Vasiljkovic (aka: Daniel Snedden). There is a strong evidence that "Vasiljkovic operated with his paramilitary death squads in eastern Bosnia until at least 1994"."

An Australian judge has found in a civil case that Serbian fugitive Captain Dragan Vasiljkovic (also known as Daniel Snedden) sought for extradition by Croatia over his wartime actions in the 1990s committed war crimes.

NSW Supreme Court judge Megan Latham said that evidence of "truthful and reliable witnesses" had established that Dragan Vasiljkovic (Daniel Snedden) "committed torture and the war crime of torture".

The judge also accepted that a Bosnian woman from Zvornik who testified in the Sydney court had correctly identified Vasiljkovic as the person who repeatedly raped her. Zvornik is located in the Srebrenica region (two municipalities are

just several miles apart).

Captain Dragan was a founder and leader of the extremist Serbian paramilitary unit called the *Knindže*. The unit operated in the forcibly occupied Croatian territories of now defunct "Republic of Serbian Krajina" (RSK). The unit, originally founded by the Serbian Secret Security, also engaged in attacks on the Bosnian enclave of Bihac.

After the Srebrenica genocide, there were concerns over the recurrence of the massacre in the Bihac pocket area, where the population of Bosniaks was four times larger than in Srebrenica and which was surrounded and under attack by Bosnian Serb and Croatian Serb forces. In the "Operation Storm", the joint forces of the Croatian Army and the Army of the Republic of Bosnia-Herzegovina took control of the so called *Republic of Serbian Krajina* and broke the siege of Bihac pocket.

Despite the attempts by the Croatian Government to extradite Vasiljkovic for prosecution and despite the judge's verdict against him, Vasiljkovic is still a free man - enjoying his life in the community (at least for now).

In September, the Bosnian ambassador to Australia Damir Arnaut told *The Sunday Age* in Sarajevo that he is gathering evidence against Vasiljkovic and that his possible extradition to Bosnia would be one of his top priorities. Arnaut said there is also strong evidence that "Vasiljkovic operated with his paramilitary death squads in eastern Bosnia until at least 1994". He noted that:

"Bosnia's court dealing with war crimes is staffed with international judges and prosecutors and it has received very high marks on the international level for its professionalism and impartiality. As a result, I plan to work with Australian and Croatian authorities to collect evidence for forwarding to Bosnian prosecutors with hope that they will bring charges against Vasiljkovic and request his extradition to Bosnia. Bosnia's court dealing with war crimes is staffed with international judges and prosecutors and it has received very high marks on the international level for its professionalism and impartiality."

THE Supreme Court is satisfied he committed the war crime of torture, participated in organised rape and admitted committing a massacre during the Balkans war. But Daniel Snedden is free in the community despite attempts by the Croatian Government to extradite him for prosecution.

Also known as Dragan Vasiljkovic or Captain Dragan, he is accused of war crimes while commanding a Serb paramilitary unit in Croatia in the early 1990s and sued for defamation after *The Australian* reported in 2005 on his alleged conduct during the conflict.

The newspaper's publisher, Nationwide News, defended the case on the grounds of truth. In the Supreme Court yesterday, Justice Megan Latham found a string of imputations were "substantially true" and Mr Snedden "was loose with the truth when it suited his purposes".

"The systematic abuse, humiliation and deprivation visited upon those whom the plaintiff sought to punish and subdue at the Knin fortress, the old hospital prison and the Sremska Mitrovika prison, was consistent with the plaintiff's stated aim to drive out non-Serbs from the Krajina [frontier]," Justice Latham said. "The accounts of electrocution, regular beatings and mock executions, carried out at the behest of, or with the authority of, the plaintiff, were harrowing."

Advertisement

Mr Snedden has strenuously denied the allegations. Outside the court, he described them as false. He intends to appeal.

Several former prisoners gave evidence in court of being kicked or beaten by Captain Dragan, or violently assaulted by military men in his presence, after being taken to his fortress at Knin. Electric shocks were administered at a nearby hospital, where guards referred to Dragan as their commander. One man recalled Dragan standing by in silence as he was attacked with batons and the handle of a broken shovel.

A woman known only as Source A gave evidence that in 1992, she was taken to a hotel in Zvornik and told to wait for "the prince", before the plaintiff raped her repeatedly.

The court also heard evidence from the *Herald's* chief foreign correspondent, Paul McGeough, who interviewed Captain Dragan at Knin in 1991. He questioned him about an earlier published quote attributed to him: "When the Croat side uses hospitals or police stations in their villages as fortified positions, I'm sorry, I just have to massacre them." Justice Latham accepted that there was no denial or clarification of the statement by the plaintiff and the imputation he committed a massacre was "substantially true".

The Republic of Croatia has sought to extradite Mr Snedden, who spent more than three years in custody without charge following his arrest. But in September the full bench of the Federal Court ordered his release, finding there was "a substantial or real chance of prejudice" if he was sent to Croatia to face prosecution for alleged war crimes. The Commonwealth will seek special leave to appeal to the High Court against the decision.

Effects of torture

The consequences of torture reach far beyond immediate pain. Many victims suffer from post-traumatic stress disorder (PTSD), which includes symptoms such as flashbacks (or intrusive thoughts), severe anxiety, insomnia, nightmares, depression and memory lapses.

Torture victims often feel guilt and shame, triggered by the humiliation they have endured. Many feel that they have betrayed themselves or their friends and family. All such symptoms are normal human responses to abnormal and inhuman treatment.

When most people think of torture, the first thing that comes to mind is unimaginable, unendurable pain. Physical pain is, however, the one thing that tends to remain in the torture chamber, the hidden cells of illegal prisons after the victim has left. As terrible as the physical after effects of torture may be, the real horror is what remains in the mind.

Unfortunately, and in spite of the United Nations, Amnesty international and the Geneva Convention, torture is still practiced all over the world today, most often by all kinds of governments, may they be democratically elected or not:

Torture is widely practiced throughout the world. Recent studies indicate that 50% of all countries, including 79% of the G-20 countries, continue to practice systematic torture despite a universal ban. (Carinci, 2010)

Perceptions of horror vary depending on contextual elements. For example, institutionalized torture that comes from within one´s own country is experienced very differently from isolated acts of torture perpetrated by non-state criminals. A feeling of helplessness is central to the torture cycle, according to Metin Besoglu, one of the world´s leading experts on the subject of torture and mass violence trauma, and this helplessness is much more dramatic in a situation where an individual knows he is facing an all-powerful enemy, such as the state or a terror regime.

Studies by Besoglu and his collaborators have also determined that political activists tend to suffer more attenuated psychological trauma. This is due to the fact that a strong belief in ideas or a solid religious faith seems to make the individual´s feel less powerless in front of the victimizers, and the feeling that one is not in control has been demonstrated to be one of the prime stressors of torture, and ultimately, a prime cause for its severely traumatizing effects.

While some earlier research tried to identify a "torture syndrome," the current literature suggests that there isn´t sufficient evidence for this, and that the disorders associated with torture experiences can be classed under the PTSD (post-traumatic stress disorder) and CTD (cumulative trauma disorders) umbrella.

In his article *Surviving Torture*, after having tended to thousands of torture survivors all over the world, Mollica advises that the focus on PTSD often makes physicians forget that the main problem encountered in this population is depression, while he also observes that professionals are sometimes afraid to ask the right questions, because they are perhaps not sure how to deal with the information about such traumatic events, or they are afraid of "opening a Pandora´s box."

In fact, post-torture symptoms range from the prevalent chronic pain, which is often connected to actual musculoskeletal damage, to neurophysiological damage associated to head injury, trauma congruent hallucinations and anhedonia. Family trauma is also very common; for example, it has been shown that children of tortured parents reveal more psychosomatic symptoms, headaches, depression, learning difficulties and aggressive behavior They manifest more severe ADHD, enuresis, and trauma related psychotic symptoms, developmental arrest or delays.

Surprisingly enough, research has also put forward the notion that torture survivors display some positive psychological traits, when compared to control groups. Namely, they are better equipped to grow out of the traumatic experience, more resilient and more tolerant to adversity than those who haven´t suffered tortured, while involved in the same violent environment. This is again attributed to the commitment to a collective cause and the presence of a strong belief system.

Behavioral intervention, including exposure to those situations which foster fear, has been seen to obtain very positive effects, such as PTSD and depression reduction, after even one single session. Surprisingly again, this has been the case even when the treatment takes place while the subjects are still living in an environment where they may still risk being tortured.

These findings come from a study of former Yugoslavia war survivors, which also indicated that redress and the reinstitution of a sense of justice in the world are not enough of themselves to significantly help torture survivors` psychological healing process. According to this paper by Besoglu and collaborators, regardless of any political and judicial changes that benefit the victims, "recovery from PTSD appears to require specific interventions designed to enhance sense of control over traumatic stressors" (Abildgaard, 1984).

In his article *You can´t fight violence with violence*, Besoglu explains how the trauma of torture and other types of mass violence commonly beget more violence. According to the same study of former Yugoslavia conflict victims, the greatest desire for vengeance was seen in people who had had loved ones tortured, raped, killed or imprisoned. Besoglu explains these violent instincts as follows:

Retaliatory aggression attenuates the feelings of helplessness that arise from trauma. For an intuitive understanding of those feelings, simply imagine your home suddenly being raided by invading forces and your loved ones being humiliated, imprisoned, tortured, raped or killed.

It would seem that, as if it wasn´t bad enough of itself, torture can not only destroy a family, and even a whole generation (i.e. during the Latin American dictatorships of the 1970´s), it is also a seed for new violence, planted on extremely fertile ground.

References

Carinci AJ, Mehta P, & Christo PJ (2010). Chronic pain in torture victims. *Current pain and headache reports, 14* (2), 73-9 PMID: 20425195

Abildgaard U, Daugaard G, Marcussen H, Jess P, Petersen HD, & Wallach M (1984). Chronic organic psycho-syndrome in Greek torture victims. *Danish medical bulletin, 31* (3), 239-42 PMID: 6744953

Mollica, R. (2004). Surviving Torture *New England Journal of Medicine, 351* (1), 5-7 DOI:10.1056/NEJMp048141

Kira, I. (2002). Torture Assessment and Treatment: The Wraparound Approach *Traumatology, 8* (2), 54-86 DOI: 10.1177/153476560200800203

Basoglu, M. (2005). Psychiatric and Cognitive Effects of War in Former Yugoslavia: Association of Lack of Redress for Trauma and Posttraumatic Stress Reactions *JAMA: The Journal of the American Medical Association, 294* (5), 580-590 DOI: 10.1001/jama.294.5.580

Kira, I., Templin, T., Lewandowski, L., Clifford, D., Wiencek, P., Hammad, A., Mohanesh, J., & Al-haidar, A. (2006). The Effects of Torture: Two Community Studies *Peace and Conflict: Journal of Peace Psychology, 12* (3), 205-228 DOI: 10.1207/s15327949pac1203_1

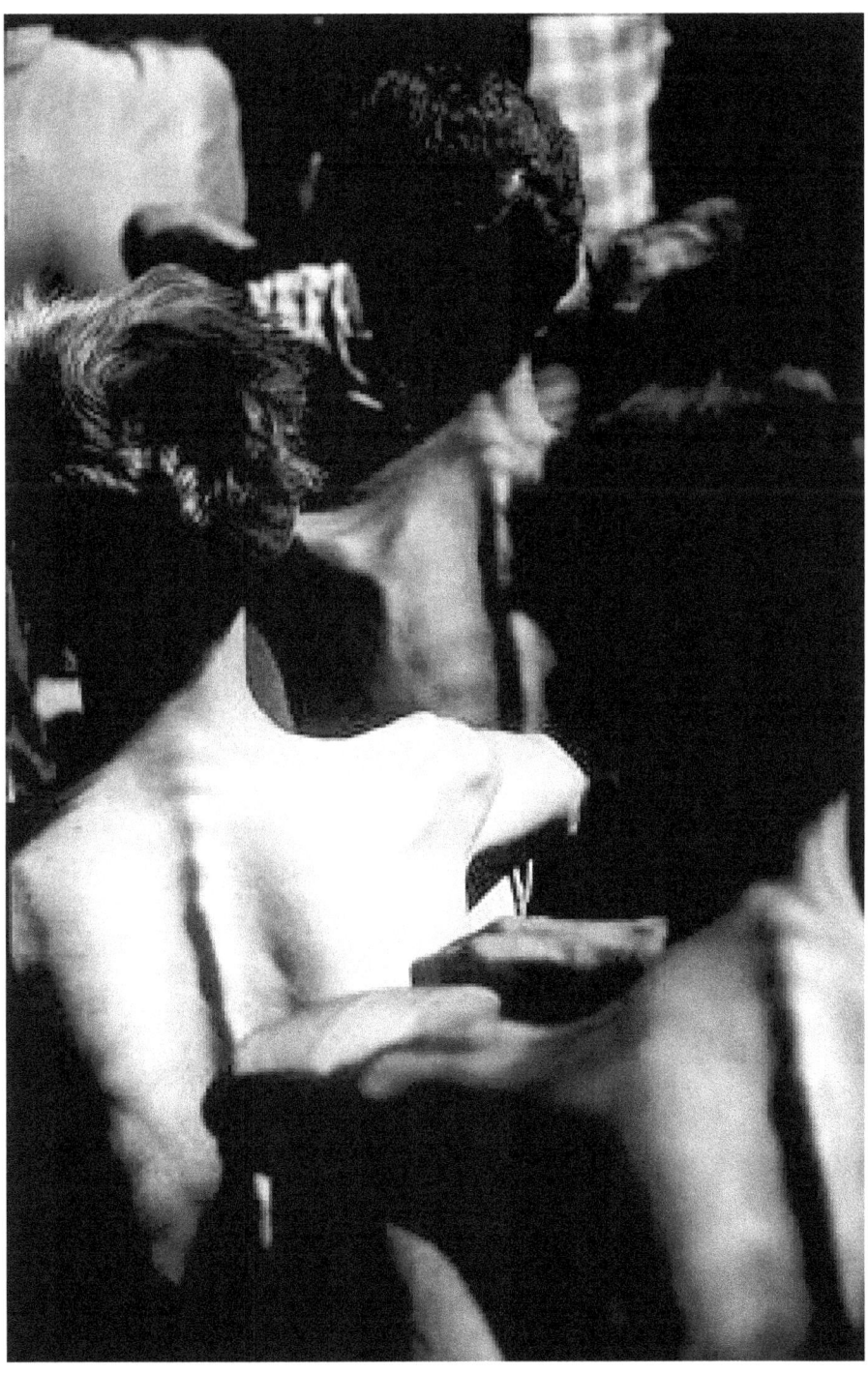

Copyright © Hakimi bin Abdul Jabar (3 June 2016)

© Abominable Atrocities - The Systematic Rape of Bosniak/Bosnian Muslim Women : Conclusive Deliberate Genocidal Crime (Arguments & Opinions)

Photo taken by **Anthony Lloyd**, noted war photographer. Image used for *Fair Use Only* and for research and educational purposes.

The International Criminal Tribunal for the former Yugoslavia (ICTY) declared that "systematic rape", and "sexual enslavement" in time of war was a crime against humanity, second only to the war crime of genocide. Although the ICTY did not treat the mass rapes as genocide, many scholars such as Becirevic, Cohen, Boose, Johan Vetlesen etc. have provided sufficient arguments and concluded from the organized, and systematic nature of the mass rapes of the female Bosniak (Bosnian Muslim) population, that these rapes were a part of a larger campaign of genocide and that the VRS were carrying out a policy of genocidal rape against the Bosnian Muslim ethnic group. Utmost due respect is given to the decision of the ICTY.

Fallout

Survivors of sexualized violence were supposed to receive property restitution and return to their former homes as long as the return would be "safe and dignified," according to the peace agreement known as the Dayton Accords that was signed after the war. However, no rules have been put in place to provide alternatives for the many women whose former homes are the site of extreme trauma and sometimes months of repeated rape, Amnesty International reported in 2009. In some cases, they are forced to return to communities full of the very neighbors who committed abuses against them and their families. In 2006, Bosnia-Herzegovina instituted a law that included a section saying that "homes should be provided for victims of sexual torture during the war," but the Ministry for Human Rights and Refugees stated that it is "not clear who should implement the act, and there is no agency making sure the law is enforced."

Legal Precedents

The International Criminal Tribunal for the Former Yugoslavia was the first international tribunal in Europe to convict for rape as a crime against humanity (following Akayesu in Rwanda). According to the ICTY website, it was also "the first international criminal tribunal to enter convictions for rape as a form of torture and for sexual enslavement as crime against humanity."

How Sexualized Violence Is Used as a Weapon of War

For ethnic cleansing: There are testimonies from women who had soldiers tell them, while raping them, that they wanted to get them pregnant or force them to have children who would look ethnically different from their mother, or that they were raping them to punish them for being Muslim (or Croatian). There were also women who became pregnant and were forced to carry their babies to term.

The U.N. defines ethnic cleansing as "a purposeful policy designed by one ethnic or religious group to remove by violent and terror-inspiring means the civilian population of another ethnic or religious group from certain geographic areas." We are using the term here because ethnic cleansing not only makes women subject to outright murder, but also controls the threat of their bodies as the means of reproduction. For instance, women have been raped in order to occupy "inferior" wombs with "superior" sperm; in other conflicts, women are forced to have abortions or sterilizations (as have men of "inferior" groups) in order to end future reproduction. As in the case of Bosnia, women are also subject to the sex-specific political torture of forcing them to bear the child of their torturer in order to break their will.

To humiliate: Many women were raped in front of their children and husbands, who were forced to watch at gunpoint; there are also a fair number of accounts of elderly women who were raped (in those cases, it was clearly not about impregnating them but about demeaning them and their families). Thousands of males were forced to engage in sexual acts with other males, including, according to some accounts, their own father or son.

To instill fear: Public rape was used to prompt the "flight or expulsion of entire Muslim communities," according to a 2006 U.N. Population Fund briefing paper. Many women were raped, sometimes repeatedly, in front of family members in their homes. Others were raped in public, outdoors, in broad daylight.

To gain information: Women have testified that before being raped they were asked for the whereabouts of men hiding in the forests. One said that soldiers waved a photograph of her boyfriend at her before raping her.

As part of looting: Rape often occurred alongside theft of private property, the U.N. Commission of Experts found in their final report on sexualized violence in the former Yugoslavia: "…[P]eople would break into homes, steal property, and torture and sexually assault the inhabitants, oftentimes in front of other family members or the public." Some testimonies refer to men rifling through houses in search of money or jewelry.

Peer pressure: Some Serbian soldiers said their peers forced them to rape when they did not wish to participate. There is at least one account of a soldier who said he felt extreme regret but had been "made to rape" by other soldiers.

Patterns of Violence

- Rape was committed by all sides but overwhelmingly by Serbs against Muslim (Bosniak) women.
- Some women were detained and raped repeatedly by many different soldiers over longer periods of time; some died of repeated rape. Rape camps were set up in restaurants, motels, schools, and other large buildings. One of the most well-known rape camps was Partizan Sports Hall, where more than 70 women were held captive and tortured for months on end.
- Apartments kept by soldiers were often sites of violence. Women and young girls were captured and transported to these homes in order to be raped and abused. Sometimes, women and girls were taken by force from a larger rape camp, such as Partizan Sports Hall, brought to a particular soldier's home, and attacked, only to be returned to the Sports Hall to suffer more sexualized violence.
- Families were also locked in their own homes and raped repeatedly alongside family members (see "Testimonies").
- Young girls, adults, and elderly women were all raped. Testimonies of elders show that these women often thought themselves to be safe due to their age and therefore did not flee, only to find that they were attacked along with the younger women.

Numbers

Reports range from 20,000 to 60,000 rapes; unfortunately, most sources state that the numbers are too hard to determine. According to one source, the U.N.'s Special Representative on Sexual Violence in Conflict, Margot Wallström, estimates there to be 50,000 to 60,000 cases. An Amnesty report states:

"There are no reliable statistics on the number of women and men who were raped or were subjected to other forms of sexual violence. Early estimates by the BiH [Bosnia and Herzegovina] government suggested the number of 50,000 victims although this estimate was questioned as unreliable and politicized. The Parliamentary Assembly of the Council of Europe estimated that 20,000 women were subjected to rape and other forms of sexual violence. The real number of those who were raped during the 1992-1995 armed conflict will probably never be established."

A U.N. report from 1994 states: "According to the State Commission in Bosnia and Herzegovina, approximately 25,000 victims had been registered," but does not explain this registration process. In addition, the report's numbers would seem to pre-date the mass rape at Srebrenica, which didn't occur until 1995. Some experts believe that the emphasis in the early 1990s on figuring out a more accurate estimate was harmful in that it allowed journalists and leaders to speculate that the issue didn't "count" as much if the numbers were lower.

Cultural Gender Attitudes

After the rapes occurred, married women were often shunned by their husbands for religious or cultural reasons. However, there was a very strong and unique movement in the region: Imams and other male Muslim community leaders encouraged husbands to set aside religious sentiments regarding raped women and take their wives back and support them more as war survivors than as irrevocably marred. It was rather specific to this conflict that rape was seen as a community problem. In addition, Indira Kajosevic, a Bosnian expert, survivor, and founder of some of the first trauma centers and feminist groups in Bosnia, says that women in the region were able to gain status through organizing in a way that was unique to this conflict.

Rape during the Bosnian War

During the Bosnian War, and the Bosnian genocide, the violence assumed a gender-targeted form through the use of rape. While men from all ethnic groups committed rape, the great majority of rapes were perpetrated by Bosnian Serb forces of the Army of the Republika Srpska (VRS) and Serb paramilitary units, who used genocidal rape as an instrument of terror as part of their programme of ethnic cleansing.[1][2][3] Estimates of the total number of women raped during the war vary. The European Union estimates a total of 20,000, while the Bosnian Interior Ministry claims 50,000.[4] The UN Commission of Experts identified 1,600 cases of rape, while experts connected to UNHRC provided evidence of 12,000 rapes.[5] Other estimates range from 12,000 to 50,000.[6][7]

The International Criminal Tribunal for the former Yugoslavia (ICTY) declared that "systematic rape", and "sexual enslavement" in time of war was a crime against humanity, second only to the war crime of genocide. Although the ICTY did not treat the mass rapes as genocide, many have concluded from the organized, and systematic nature of the mass rapes of the female Bosniak (Bosnian Muslim) population, that these rapes were a part of a larger campaign of genocide,[8][9][10] and that the VRS were carrying out a policy of genocidal rape against the Bosnian Muslim ethnic group.[11]

The trial of VRS member Dragoljub Kunarac was the first time in any national or international jurisprudence that a person was convicted of using rape as a weapon of war. The widespread media coverage of the atrocities by Serbian paramilitary and military forces against Bosniak women and children, drew international condemnation of the Serbian forces.[12][13]

Following the war, several award-winning documentaries and feature films were produced which cover the rapes and their aftermath.

Rape as genocidal crime

Excavation of a mass grave in eastern Bosnia. Civilian men from Foča were executed whilst women were detained and repeatedly raped by members of the Bosnian Serb armed forces.

According to Amnesty International, the use of rape during times of war is not a by-product of conflicts, but a pre-planned and deliberate military strategy.[14] The Rape of Nanking has been described by Adam Jones as "one of the most savage instances of genocidal rape". The violence saw tens of thousands of women gang raped and killed.[15] In the last quarter of a century, the majority of conflicts have shifted from wars between nation states to communal and intrastate civil wars. During these conflicts the use of rape as a weapon against the civilian population by state and non-state actors has become more frequent. Journalists and human rights organizations have documented campaigns of genocidal rape during the conflicts in the Balkans, Sierra Leone, Rwanda, Liberia, Sudan, Uganda, and the Democratic Republic of the Congo. John Y. Lee argues that a similar tribunal to the ICTY be formed to prosecute the Japanese armed forces for their use of "comfort women" during World War II.[16] The strategic aims of these mass rapes are twofold. The first is to instill terror in the civilian population, with the intent to forcibly dislocate them from their property. The second is to reduce the likelihood of return and reconstitution by inflicting humiliation and shame on the targeted population. These effects are strategically important for non-state actors, as it is necessary for them to remove the targeted population from the land. The use of mass rape is well suited for campaigns which involve ethnic cleansing and genocide, as the objective is to destroy or forcefully remove the target population, and ensure they do not return.[17]

Background

The war-torn Sarajevo neighborhood of Grbavica in 1996, a site of rape camps during the Bosnian War and subject of the award-winning film Grbavica.[18]

Historians such as Niall Ferguson have assessed a key factor behind the high-level decision to use mass rape for ethnic cleansing as being misguided nationalism.[19] Prior to 1980, it is widely believed that the lack of ethnic conflict in Yugoslavia was due to nationalism being effectively repressed by Marshal Tito.[20] In 1989 Serbian president, Slobodan Milošević inflamed Serbian nationalist sentiment with the Gazimestan Speech which referred to the Battle of Kosovo.[21][22] Feelings of victimhood and aggression towards Bosniaks were further stirred up with exaggerated tales about the role played by a small number of Bosniaks in the persecution of Serbs during the Ustaše genocide in the 1940s.[23] Serb propaganda suggested that Bosniaks were racially different, typically that they were actually of largely Turkish blood,[24] when in fact DNA tests have shown both groups to share the same gene pool.[25] Despite the Serbian government-led hate campaigns, some Serbs tried to defend Bosniaks from the atrocities and had to be threatened, including instances when troops would announce by loud speaker that "every Serb who protects a Muslim will be killed immediately".[19]

Before the conflict began, Bosniaks in Eastern Bosnia had already begun to be removed from their employment, to be ostracised and to have their freedom of movement curtailed. At the outset of the war, Serb forces began to target the Bosniak civilian population.[26] Once towns and villages were secured, the military, the police, the paramilitaries and, sometimes, even Serb villagers continued these attacks. Bosniak houses and apartments were looted or razed to the ground, the civilian population were rounded up, some were physically abused or murdered during the process. Men and women were separated and then held in concentration camps.[27]

Occurrences of rape

Estimates of the number of women and girls raped range from 12,000 to 50,000, the vast majority of whom were Bosniaks raped by Bosnian Serbs.[6][7] The Serb forces set up "rape camps", where women were subjected to being repeatedly raped, and only released when pregnant.[7] Gang rape and public rapes in front of villagers and neighbors were not uncommon.[28]

On 6 October 1992 the United Nations Security Council established a Commission of Experts chaired by M. Cherif Bassiouni. According to the commission's findings, it was apparent that rape was being used by Serb forces systematically, and had the support of commanders and local authorities.[a] The commission also reported that some perpetrators said they were ordered to rape. Others said that the use of rape was a tactic to make sure the targeted population would not return to the area. The assailants told their victims they would bear a child of the assailant's ethnicity. Pregnant women were detained until it was too late to have the fetus aborted. Victims were told they would be hunted down and killed should they report what had transpired.[30] The commission also concluded that: "Rape has been reported to have been committed by all sides to the conflict. However, the largest number of reported victims have been Bosniaks, and the largest number of alleged perpetrators have been Bosnian Serbs. There are few reports of rape and sexual assault between members of the same ethnic group."[31]

The team of European Community investigators, including Simone Veil and Anne Warburton, similarly concluded in their 1993 report that rape carried out by the Bosnian Serb forces was not a secondary effect of the conflict but part of a systematic policy of ethnic cleansing and was "perpetrated with the conscious intention of demoralizing and terrorizing communities, driving them from their home regions and demonstrating the power of the invading forces".[32] Amnesty International and Helsinki Watch also concluded during the conflict that rape was being used as a weapon of war, with the primary purpose being to cause humiliation, degradation, and intimidation to ensure the survivors would leave and never return.[33][34]

Throughout the conflict, women of all ethnic groups were affected, although not on the scale that the Bosniak population suffered.[6]

Testimony from a survivor of the Kalinovik camp, where roughly 100 women had been detained and subjected to MPR, the rapists continually told their victims, "You are going to have our children. You are going to have our little Chetniks", and that the reason for their being raped was to "plant the seed of Serbs in Bosnia". Women were forced to go full term with their pregnancies and give birth.[35] Many of the reports of the abuses illustrated the ethnic dimension of the rapes.[b]

Locations and procedures

"Karaman's House", a location where women were tortured and raped near Foča, Bosnia and Herzegovina. (Photograph provided courtesy of the ICTY)

Serb forces set up camps where rapes occurred, such as those at Keraterm,[37][c] Vilina Vlas, Manjača,[39] Omarska, Trnopolje, Uzamnica and Vojno.[40] In May 1992, Serb villagers from Snagovo, Zvornik, surrounded and captured the village of Liplje and turned it into a concentration camp. Four-hundred people were imprisoned in a few houses and those held there were subject to rape, torture and murder.[41]

Over a five-month period between the spring and summer of 1992, between 5,000 and 7,000 Bosniaks and Croats were held in inhumane conditions at Omarska.[42] At the concentration camp, rape, sexual assaults and torture of men and women were commonplace. One newspaper described the events there as "the location of an orgy of killing, mutilation, beating and rape".[43][44] rape murder and physical abuse were commonplace.[45] At the Trnopolje camp an unknown number of women and girls were raped by Bosnian Serb soldiers, police officers and the camp guards.[46] At the Uzamnica camp, one witness in the trial of Oliver Krsmanovic, charged with crimes relating to the Višegrad massacres, claimed that the male detainees were at one time forced to rape women.[47]

Detention camps were set up across the Serb-controlled town of Foča. While kept at one of the town's most notable rape locations, "Karaman's house", Bosniak females, including minors as young as 12, were repeatedly raped.[48] During the trial of Dragoljub Kunarac et al., the conditions of these camps were described as being "intolerably unhygienic", and the head of the police in Foča, Dragan Gagović, was identified as being one of the men who would visit these camps, where he would select women, take them outside, and then rape them.[d]

Women and girls selected by Kunarac, or by his men, were taken to the soldiers' base and raped. At other times, girls were removed from detention centers and kept in various locations for prolonged periods of time under sexual slavery.[50] Radomir Kovač, who was also convicted by the ICTY, personally kept four girls in his apartment, abusing and raping three of them many times, while also allowing acquaintances to rape one of the girls. Prior to selling three of the girls, Kovač appointed two of them to other Serb soldiers who abused them for more than three weeks.[51]

Croat forces set up concentration camps at, Čelebići, Dretelj, Gabela, Rodoč, Kaonik, Vitez, and Žepa.[40] At the Čelebići facility, Serb civilians were subjected to various forms of torture and sexual abuse, including rape.[52] At Dretelj the majority of prisoners were Serbian civilians, who were held in inhumane conditions, while female detainees were raped and told that they would be held until they gave birth to an "Ustaša".[53] Both Serbian and Bosniak civilians were held at the Heliodrom camp in Rodoc, and detainees were reported to have been sexually assaulted.[54]

In Doboj, Bosnian Serb forces separated the females from the men and then facilitated the rape of some women by their own male family members. Women were questioned as to male relatives in the city, and one woman's fourteen-year-old son was forced to rape her."[55] Some writers have expressed skepticism about men's claims to have been forced to rape in such situations, arguing that once their penises became erect, they were active participants in the rape, regardless of other circumstances.[56] These arguments are likely a direct cause of the under reporting of sexual violence by male victims.

Aftermath

Following the end of hostilities with the 1995 Dayton Agreement, there have been sustained efforts to reconcile the opposing factions.[57] Much attention has been paid to the need to understand the reality of what happened during the war, dispel myths, and for responsible leaders to be brought to justice and be encouraged to accept their guilt for the mass rapes and other atrocities.[58]

In the aftermath of the conflict, ethnic identity is now of much greater social importance in Bosnia than it was prior to 1992. From the 1960s until the beginning of the war, nearly twelve percent of marriages were mixed (between members of different communities), and young citizens would often refer to themselves as Bosnians rather than identifying their ethnicity. After the conflict it has been effectively mandatory to be identified as either Bosniak, Serb or Croat and this has been a problem for the children of rape victims as they come of age.[59]

A medical study of 68 Croatian and Bosniak victims of rape during the 1992–1995 war found that many suffered psychological problems as a result. None had any psychiatric history prior to the rapes. After the rapes 25 had suicidal thoughts, 58 suffered depression immediately after and 52 were still suffering from depression at the time of the study, one year later. Of the women 44 had been raped more than once and 21 of them had been raped daily throughout their captivity. Twenty-nine of them had become pregnant and seventeen had an abortion. The study reached the conclusion that the rapes had "deep immediate and long-term consequences on the mental-health" of the women.[60]

In the study entitled "Mass Rape: The War Against Women in Bosnia-Herzegovina", Alexandra Stiglmayer et al. conclude:[61]

In Bosnia-Herzegovina and Croatia, rape has been an instrument of 'ethnic cleansing'. The UN Commission of experts that investigated the rapes in former Yugoslavia has concluded. 'Rape cannot be seen as incidental to the main purpose of the aggression but as serving a strategic purpose in itself,' reports the European Community mission concerned especially with the situation of Bosniak women.The report of the humanitarian organization Amnesty International states: 'Instances that have included sexual infringements against women are apparently part of an inclusive pattern of war conduct characterized by massive intimidation and infringements against Bosniaks and Croats.' The

American human rights organization Helsinki Watch believes that rape is being used as a 'weapon of war' in Bosnia-Herzegovina: ' Whether a woman is raped by soldiers in her home or is held in a house with other women and raped over and over again, she is raped with a political purpose – to intimidate, humiliate, and degrade her and others affected by her suffering. The effect of rape is often to ensure that women and their families will flee and never return.' Against this background, it is obvious that rapes in Bosnia-Herzegovina are taking place 'on a large scale' (UN and EC), that they are acquiring a systematic character, and that 'in by far the most instances Muslim (Bosniak) women are the victims of the Serbian forces' (Amnesty International). Estimates of the number of rape victims range from 20,000 (EC) to 50,000 (Bosnian Ministry of the Interior)."

National and International reactions

In August 1992 media stories publicized the use of rape as a war strategy,[62] and one of the first to bring it to the world's attention was Newsday correspondent Roy Gutman's programme Mass Rape: Muslims Recall Serb Attacks, which aired on August 23 1992.[63]

The United Nations Security Council established the ICTY in response to the conflict's human rights violations.[64] Article 5 of the ICTY charter clarified that the tribunal had the power to prosecute war crimes, and the charter specifically condemned rape as a crime, for which people could be indicted.[16]

A Central Intelligence Agency report leaked in 1995 stated that Serb forces were responsible for 90 percent of the atrocities committed during the conflict.[65] A report compiled by a team of experts for the UN, chaired by M. Cherif Bassiouni, reached the same conclusion, calculating that Croat forces were responsible for six percent of the atrocities and Bosniak forces for four percent.[66]

After the fall of Srebrenica in July 1995, Madeleine Albright, the U.S. Ambassador to the United Nations, told the UN Security Council that "[the] whereabouts of some 6,000 Bosniak men and boys from Srebrenica was unknown. But their fate was not. We have enough information to conclude now, however, that the Bosnian Serbs beat, raped, and executed many of the refugees"[67]

Legal proceedings

The Tribunal building in The Hague.

In the early 1990s, calls were made for legal action to be taken over the possibility of genocide having occurred in Bosnia. The ICTY set the precedent that rape in warfare is a form of torture. By 2011, it had indicted 161 people from all ethnic backgrounds for war crimes,[68] and heard evidence from over 4,000 witnesses.[69] In 1993, the ICTY defined rape as a crime against humanity, and also defined rape, sexual slavery, and sexual violence as international crimes which constitute torture and genocide.[70]

Judges from the ICTY ruled during the trial of Dragoljub Kunarac, Radomir Kovač and Milorad Krnojelac that rape had been used by the Bosnian Serb armed forces as an "instrument of terror".[71] Kunarac was sentenced to 28 years' imprisonment for rape, torture and enslaving women.[72] Kovač, who had raped a 12-year-old child and then sold her into slavery,[73] was sentenced to 20 years imprisonment and Krnojelac to 15 years.[74] The ICTY declared that a "hellish orgy of persecution" had occurred in various camps across Bosnia.[71]

In 1997, Radovan Karadžić was sued by Bosniak and Croat women in an American court for genocidal rape. He was tried and convicted in absentia. The female plaintiffs were found to be victims of genocidal rape, and awarded 745 million dollars in damages.[75][76]

On 26 June 1996, the ICTY indicted Dragan Zelenović on seven counts of rape and torture as crimes against humanity, and seven counts of rape and torture as violations of the customs and laws of war. Zelenović initially plead not guilty, but during a hearing on 17 December 2007, the trial chamber accepted a guilty plea on three counts of torture and four counts of rape as crimes against humanity. Zelenović had taken part in the sexual assaults of women at various camps, including the gang rape of a 15-year-old girl and an adult woman. He was given a 15-year sentence for crimes against humanity, which he appealed. The appeal chamber upheld the original sentence.[77]

On 10 March 1997, in what is best known as the Čelebići case, Hazim Delić, Zejnil Delalić, Zdravko Mucić and Esad Landžo were put on trial. They were charged under article 7(1)[e] and article 7(3)[f] of the ICT statutes for violating international humanitarian laws. The offenses occurred in the Bosniak- and Croat-controlled Čelebići prison camp.[80] Delić was found guilty of using rape as torture, which was a breach of the Fourth Geneva Convention and that he had violated the laws and customs of war. The trial chamber also found that Mucić was guilty of crimes carried out while he was commander of the camp, under the principle of command responsibility, these included gender related atrocities.[81]

On 22 June 1998, Anto Furundžija, who had been apprehended on 18 December 1997 by Dutch forces who were operating with NATO,[82] was put on trial in what was one of the shortest trials heard by the ICTY.[83] This was the first case heard by the ICTY which dealt exclusively with charges for rape. Furundžija was a Bosnian Croat and local commander of the militia known as The Jokers, who took part in the Lašva Valley ethnic cleansing and who were under the command of the Croatian Defence Council. Furundžija was indicted for individual criminal responsibility, which included "committing, planning, instigating, ordering or otherwise aiding and abetting in the planning, preparation or execution of any crimes referred to in articles two and three of the tribunal statute."[84] A single witness, who had been assaulted by Furundžija while he interrogated her, gave the majority of testimony during this trial. She was beaten, and another soldier forced her to have oral and vaginal sex while Furundžija was present.

Furundžija did not act to prevent the assault, even though he was in a position of command. His defense counsel argued that the witness was suffering from post traumatic stress disorder and had misidentified the accused.[85] The trial chamber gave Furundžija two sentences of 10 and 8 years to run concurrently having found him guilty under article three, in that he had violated "the laws or customs of war for torture and for outrages upon personal dignity, including rape."[86]

In May 2009, Jadranko Prlić, who had been prime minister of the self-proclaimed Bosnian Croat wartime state of Herzeg-Bosnia, was convicted of murder, rape and expulsion of Bosniaks. He was sentenced to 25 years imprisonment.[87]

According to Margot Wallström, U.N. Special Representative on Sexual Violence in Conflict, only 12 cases out of an estimated 50,000 to 60,000 have been prosecuted as of 2010.[88] By April 2011 the ICTY had indicted 93 men, of these 44 were indicted for crimes related to sexual violence.[89]

On 9 March 2005, the War Crimes Chamber of the Court of Bosnia and Herzegovina, was officially inaugurated.[90] At first this was a hybrid court of international and national judges, by 2009 all judicial actions were handed over to the domestic authorities.[91]

Radovan Stanković was a member of an elite paramilitary unit from Vukovar which was commanded by Pero Elez. Following the death of

Elez, Stanković took command of Karaman's house which he ran as a brothel.[92] On 14 November 2006, the domestic court in Sarajevo tried Stanković and he was given a 16-year sentence for forcing women into prostitution. On 26 May 2007, while being transported to hospital Stankovic escaped from custody.[93]

Neđo Samardžić was given a sentence of 13 years and 4 months after he was found guilty of crimes against humanity. He had been indicted on ten counts, four of which he was found guilty of. These included multiple rape, beatings, murder, and forcing women to be sexual slaves. Samardžić was also found guilty of having committed atrocities at Karaman's house.[94] Samardžić appealed and was given 24 years imprisonment having been found guilty on nine of the ten indictments.[95]

Gojko Janković surrendered himself to the authorities in Bosnia in 2005. He was transferred to the Hague for trial but the ICTY sent him back to Bosnia to be tried before the domestic court. He was indicted for the rights violations of, aiding and abetting and issuing orders during an attack on the non-Serbian population which resulted in the killing, and sexual abuse of non-Serbians, the majority of who were Bosniak women and girls. He was given a sentence of 34 years imprisonment having been found guilty.[96]

Dragan Damjanović (24 years in prison) was convicted of war crimes including murder, torture and rape.[97]

Momir Savić was given 18 years imprisonment in July 2009 for crimes he had carried out while a commander of the Serbian armies "Višegrad Brigade". He was convicted for the repeated rape of a Bosniak woman, arson, looting and carrying out executions.[98][99]

On 12 January 2009, Željko Lelek was given 13 years imprisonment for crimes against humanity, which included rape. Lelek, who was a police officer at the time, was convicted for actions he carried out during the Višegrad massacres.[100]

Miodrag Nikačević, a police officer from Foča, was indicted by the domestic court in 2007 for crimes against humanity carried out in 1992. The indictment against him were for two counts of rape. In April 1992, Nikačević, who was in uniform and armed, forcibly robbed and raped one woman. The second charge was for the abuse of and rape of another woman in July 1992 in Foča.[101] During the trial, the defense produced ten witnesses who claimed that Nikačević had not taken part in any war crimes, and had at times risked his own safety to help others.[102] He was found guilty on 19 February 2009 and sentenced to 8 years imprisonment for the rapes of both women, and for aiding and abetting in the abduction and illegal detention of a Bosniak civilian, who was later killed at an undisclosed location.[103] Milorad Krnojelac, Janko Janjić, Dragan Gagović and others were indicted in 1992 for human rights violations committed during the ethnic cleansing of Foča. The indictment included a charge of rape.[104]

Ante Kovač, who was a commander of the military police in the Croat Defence Council, was indicted on 25 March 2008 on war crimes carried out against Bosniaks in the municipality of Vitez in 1993. The charges included allegations of rapes carried out at detention camps in the region.[105] Kovač was cleared on one count of rape but found guilty on another. He was sentenced to 9 years imprisonment.[106]

Veselin Vlahović, also known as "Batko" or the "Monster of Grbavica", was sentenced to 45 years' imprisonment in March 2013, having been found guilty on more than sixty counts, including the murder, rape and torture of Bosniak and Croat civilians during the Siege of Sarajevo.[107] Vlahović's sentence was the longest handed down, slightly longer than that of Sanko Kojić, who—earlier in 2013—had been sentenced to 43 years' imprisonment for his role in the Srebrenica massacre.[108]

In popular culture

Calling the Ghosts is a documentary about a Bosniak woman and a Croat woman, who both survived being raped and tortured at Omarska.[109][110] The film ends with the two women giving testimony at the Hague.[111] The 1998 war film Savior is about an American mercenary escorting a Serb woman to a UN safe area after she has been raped and impregnated by a Bosniak soldier.[112] Grbavica is a feature film directed by Jasmila Žbanić. It is set in post-war Sarajevo and focuses on Esma, a single mother, and Sara, her daughter, who discovers she is a war baby as her mother had been raped. The film won the 2006 Golden Bear award at the 56th Berlin International Film Festival.[113] Žbanić had also written and directed a short documentary about the war in 2000, titled Red Rubber Boots.[114] I Came to Testify is a documentary by PBS which covers the story of sixteen women who were imprisoned by Serb forces in Foča, and who later testified against their assailants at the ICTY.[115] In the Land of Blood and Honey, directed by Angelina Jolie, also deals with the subject of wartime rape.[116][117]

"In Bosnia, some of the reported rape and sexual assault cases committed by Serbs, mostly against Muslims, are clearly the result of individual or small group conduct without evidence of command direction or an overall policy. However, many more seem to be a part of an overall pattern whose characteristics include: similarities among practices in non-contiguous geographic areas; simultaneous commission of other international humanitarian law violations; simultaneous military activity; simultaneous activity to displace civilian populations; common elements in the commission of rape, maximizing shame and humiliation to not only the victim, by also the victim's community; and the timing of the rapes. One factor in particular that leads to this conclusion is the large number of rapes which occurred in places of detention. These rape in detention do not appear to be random, and they indicate at least a policy of encouraging rape supported by the deliberate failure of camp commanders and local authorities to exercise command and control over the personnel under their authority."[29]

"The women knew the rapes would begin when Marš na Drinu was played over the loudspeaker of the main mosque. (Marš na Drinu, or

March on the Drina, is reportedly a former Chetnik fighting song that was banned during the Tito years.) While Marš na Drinu was playing, the women were ordered to strip and soldiers entered the homes taking the ones they wanted. The age of women taken ranged from 12 to 60. Frequently the soldiers would seek out mother and daughter combinations. Many of the women were severely beaten during the rapes."[36]

"At Keraterm camp, a number of guards raped a female inmate on a table in a dark room until she lost consciousness. The next morning she found herself lying in a pool of blood."[38]

Women were kept in various detention centres where they had to live in intolerably unhygienic conditions, where they were mistreated in many ways including, for many of them, being raped repeatedly. Serb soldiers or policemen would come to these detention centres, select one or more women, take them out and rape them ... All this was done in full view, in complete knowledge and sometimes with the direct involvement of the local authorities, particularly the police forces. The head of Foča police forces, Dragan Gagović, was personally identified as one of the men who came to these detention centres to take women out and rape them.[49]

"A person who orders an act or omission with the awareness of the substantial likelihood that a crime will be committed in the execution of that order, has the requisite mens rea for establishing liability under article 7(1) pursuant to ordering, Ordering with such awareness has to be regarded as accepting that crime."[78]

"A superior may be held responsible for the crimes of his subordinates, where he (a) failed to prevent the commission of those crimes, know or had reason to know that they would likely be committed, or (b) failed to punish those who committed them."[79]

References(Numbered 1 to 117)

1)   Totten & Bartrop 2007, pp. 356-57.

Henry 2010, p. 65.

Hyndman 2009, p. 204.

Ken Booth (6 December 2012). The Kosovo Tragedy: The Human Rights Dimensions. Routledge. p. 73. ISBN 978-1-136-33476-4.

Steven L. Burg; Paul S. Shoup (4 March 2015). Ethnic Conflict and International Intervention: Crisis in Bosnia-Herzegovina, 1990-93: Crisis in Bosnia-Herzegovina, 1990-93. Taylor & Francis. pp. 222–. ISBN 978-1-317-47101-1.

Wood 2013, p. 140.

Crowe 2013, p. 343.

Becirevic 2014, p. 117.

Cohen 1996, p. 47.

Boose 2002, p. 73.

Johan Vetlesen 2005, p. 197.

Stiglmayer 1994, p. 202.

Morales 2001, p. 180.

Smith-Spark 2012.

Jones 2006, p. 329.

Lee 2000, p. 160.

Leaning 2009, p. 174.

Goscilo 2012, p. 241.

Ferguson 2009, pp. 626–631.

Pelinka & Ronen 1997, p. 101.

Elsie 2004, p. 6.

Ferguson 1996, p. 627.

Ching 2008, p. 26.

Maners 2000, p. 307.

Dutton 2007, p. 37.

Burg & Shoup 2000, p. 183.

Cawthorne 2009, p. 1992.

Parrot & Cummings 2008, p. 39.

Allen 1996, p. 47.

Allen 1996, p. 77.

Allen 1996, p. 78.

Hazan 2004, p. 34.

MacKinnon 1994, p. 85.

Dombrowski 2004, p. 333.

Weitsman 2008, pp. 561-578.

Seventh Report on War Crimes in the Former Yugoslavia: Part II 1993.

Downey 2013, p. 139.

Oosthuizen 2010, p. 35.

Skjelsbæk 2006, p. 63.

Mojzes 2011, p. 172.

Becirevic 2014, p. 91.

Robinson 1998, p. 185.

Hewstone 2009, p. 73.

Henry 2010, pp. 66-67.

May 2007, p. 237.

Halilovich, Hariz (2013). Places of Pain: Forced Displacement, Popular Memory, and Trans-Local Identities in Bosnian War-Torn Communities. Berghahn Books. ISBN 978-0857457769.

Tausan, Marija (20 August 2013). "Defence Witnesses Speak about Abusers in Uzamnica". BRIN. Retrieved 6 November 2014.

McDonald & Swaak-Goldman 1999, p. 1414.

de Brouwer 2005, pp. 90-91.

Lekha Sriram et al. 2014, p. 169.

Luban 2009, p. 1173.

Walsh 2012, p. 63.

Weitsman 2007, p. 124.

Bogati 2001.

Abu-Hamad 1995, pp. 17-18.

Sander 1994, p. xix.

Malek 2005.

Boraine 2002.

Saunders 2009.

Lončar & Medved 2006, pp. 67-75.

Stiglmayer 1994, p. 85.

Carpenter 2010, p. 58.

Skjelsbæk 2006, p. 374.

de Brouwer 2005, p. 16.

Kennedy 2002, p. 252.

Waller 2002, pp. 276-277.

LeBor 2006, pp. 112-113.

Ralston & Finnin 2007, p. 54.

Lieberman 2013, pp. 229-230.

Barberet 2014, p. 111.

Simic 2014, p. 65.

Meron 2011, p. 251.

Drakulic 2013, p. 63.

Buss 2002, pp. 91-99.

Brooks 1999, p. 5.

Sjoberg & Gentry 2007, pp. 143-144.

Cengic 2009, pp. 980-981.

Van Sliedregt 2012, p. 106.

Eboe-Osuji 2007, p. 311.

Yee 2003, pp. 143-144.

Borchelt 2005, p. 307.

Williams & Scharf 1998, p. 17.

Zappala 2009, pp. 683-685.

Henry 2010, p. 109.

Henry 2010, p. 110.

Borchelt 2005, p. 308.

Escritt & Zuvela 2013.

Cerkez 2010.

Ginn 2013, p. 569.

Ivanišević 2008, p. 5.

Ivanišević 2008, p. 41.

McDonald & Swaak-Goldman 1999, p. 1414–1415.

Dewey 2008, p. 98.

Birn BiH 2006 a.

BIRN BiH 2006 b.

Haas 2013, p. 308.

Brunner 2006.

Reuters 2009.

Times Wire Reports 2009.

Becirevic 2014, p. 184.

BIRN BiH & 2008 a.

Husejnović 2009.

Zuvela 2009.

Ralston & Finnin 2007, p. 55.

BIRN BiH & 2008 b.

BIRN BiH 2010.

BBC 2013.

Al Jazeera 2013.

Senasi 2008, p. 110.

Goodman 1997.

Senasi 2008, p. 118.

Stephen Holden (25 November 1998). "In the Butchery of Bosnia, a Killer Becomes a Humanitarian". The New York Times. Retrieved 6 November 2014.

Kosmidou 2012, p. 99.

Kosmidou 2012, p. 98.

Damon 2011.

Pulver 2012.

117) Beames 2012.

Bibliography

Abu-Hamad, Aziz (1995). "Rape as a Weapon of War". The Human Rights Watch Global Report on Women's Human Rights (PDF). Human Rights Watch. ISBN 0-300-06546-9.

"Bosnia's 'Monster of Grbavica' gets 45 years". Al Jazeera. AFP. 29 March 2013. Retrieved 3 August 2014.

Allen, Beverly (1996). Rape Warfare: Hidden Genocide in Bosnia-Herzegovina and Croatia. University of Minnesota Press. ISBN 978-0-8166-2818-6.

Barberet, Rosemary L (2014). Women, Crime and Criminal Justice: A Global Enquiry. Routledge. ISBN 978-0-415-85636-2.

Beames, Robert (15 February 2012). "Berlin Film Festival: Angelina Jolie's In the Land of Blood and Honey, review". The Telegraph. Retrieved 4 August 2014.

"Bosnia jails Serb Veselin Vlahovic for war crimes". BBC. 29 March 2013. Retrieved 3 August 2014.

Becirevic, Edina (2014). Genocide on the Drina River. Yale University Press. ISBN 978-0-300-19258-2.

"Nine Years for Crimes Committed in Vite". BRIN (Justice Report). 12 November 2010. Retrieved 3 August 2014.

"Kovac charged over Vitez Crimes". BIRN (Justice Report). 25 March 2008. Retrieved 3 August 2014.

"Samardzic sentenced to 13 years". Justice Report (BIRN). 7 April 2006. Retrieved 30 July 2014.

"Nikacevic: Indictment confirmed". BIRN (Justice Report). 17 March 2008. Retrieved 3 August 2014.

"Samardzic gets 24-year jail sentence". Justice Report (BIRN BiH). 14 December 2006. Retrieved 30 July 2014.

Bogati, Vjera (28 July 2001). "Courtside: Tuta & Stela - First Mostar Crimes Heard". Institute for War & Peace Reporting. Retrieved 23 July 2014.

Boose, Lynda E. (2002). "Crossing the River Drina: Bosnian Rape Camps, Turkish Impalement, and Serb Cultural Memory". Signs (University of Chicago Press) 28 (1): 71–96. doi:10.1086/340921.

Borchelt, Gretchen (2005). "Sexual Violence Against Women in War and Armed Conflict". In Barnes, Andrea. The Handbook of Women, Psychology, and the Law (1st ed.). John Wiley & Sons. pp. 293–327. ISBN 978-0-7879-7060-4.

Boraine, Alex (18 December 2002). "Toward reconciliation : War criminal's remorse could help Bosnia heal". New York Times. Retrieved 23 July 2014.

Brooks, Roy L. (1999). "The Age of Apology". In Brooks, Roy L. When Sorry isn't Enough: The Controversy Over Apologies and Reparations for Human Injustice. New York University Press. pp. 3–12. ISBN 978-0-8147-1332-7.

Brunner, Lisl (15 December 2006). "Bosnian Serb sentenced to 20 years by war crimes court". JURIST. Retrieved 1 August 2014.

Burg, Steven L.; Shoup, Paul S. (2000). Ethnic Conflict and International Intervention: Crisis in Bosnia-Herzegovina, 1990–93 (New ed.). M.E. Sharpe. ISBN 978-1-56324-309-7.

Buss, Doris (2002). "Prosecuting Mass Rape: Prosecutor v. Dragoljub Kunarac, Radomir Kovac and Zoran Vukovic". Feminist Legal Studies 10 (1): 91–99. doi:10.1023/A:1014965414217.

de Brouwer, Anne-Marie (2005). Supranational Criminal Prosecution of Sexual Violence: The ICC and the Practice of the ICTY and the ICTR. Intersentia. ISBN 978-90-5095-533-1.

Carpenter, R. Charli (2010). Forgetting Children Born of War: Setting the Human Rights Agenda in Bosnia. Columbia University Press. ISBN 978-0-231-15130-6.

Cawthorne, Nigel (2009). The World's Ten Most Evil Men - From Twisted Dictators to Child Killers. John Blake. ISBN 978-1-84454-745-6.

Cengic, Amir (2009). "Cases". In Cassese, Antonio. The Oxford Companion to International Criminal Justice. Oxford University Press. ISBN 978-0-19-923832-3.

Cerkez, Aida (26 November 2010). "UN official: Bosnia war rapes must be prosecuted". Fox News.

Ching, Jacqueline (2008). Genocide and the Bosnian War. Rosen Publishing. ISBN 978-1-4042-1826-0.

Cohen, Philip J. (1996). "The Complicity of Serbian Intellectuals". In Cushman, Thomas; Mestrovic, Stjepan G. This Time We Knew: Western Responses to Genocide in Bosnia. New York University Press. pp. 39–65. ISBN 978-0-8147-1535-2.

Goscilo, Helena (2012). Hashamova, Yana, ed. Embracing Arms - Cultural Representation of Slavic and Balkan Women in War. Central European University Press. ISBN 978-615-5225-09-3.

Crowe, David M. (2013). War Crimes, Genocide, and Justice: A Global History. Palgrave Macmillan. ISBN 978-0-230-62224-1.

Dewey, Susan (2008). Hollow Bodies: Institutional Responses to Sex Trafficking in Armenia, Bosnia and India. Kumarian Press. ISBN 978-1-56549-265-3.

Damon, Matt (11 October 2011). "I Came to Testify". PBS. Retrieved 3 August 2014.

Drakulic, Slavenka (2013). They Would Never Hurt A Fly (1st American ed.). Viking Press. ISBN 978-0-670-03332-4.

Downey, Anthony (2013). "Exemplary Subjects: Camps and the Politics of Representation". In Frost, Tom. Giorgio Agamben: Legal, Political and Philosophical Perspectives. Routledge. p. 142. ISBN 978-0-415-63758-9.

Dutton, Donald G. (2007). The Psychology of Genocide, Massacres, and Extreme Violence: Why "Normal" People Come to Commit Atrocities (1st ed.). Praeger. ISBN 978-0-275-99000-8.

Parrot, Andrea; Cummings, Nina (2008). Sexual Enslavement of Girls and Women Worldwide. Greenwood Publishing Group. ISBN 978-0-275-99291-0.

Eboe-Osuji, Chile (2007). "Superior or Command Responsibility: A Doubtful Theory of Criminal Responsibility at the Ad Hoc Tribunals". In Decaux, Emmanuel; Dieng, Adama; Sow, Malick. Des droits de l'homme au droit international pénal (Bilingual ed.). Martinus Nijhoff. pp. 311–344. ISBN 978-90-04-16055-2.

Elsie, Robert (2004). Historical Dictionary of Kosova. Scarecrow Press. ISBN 978-0-8108-5309-6.

Escritt, Thomas; Zuvela, Maja (29 May 2013). "Bosnian Croat leaders jailed for 1990s ethnic cleansing". Reuters. Retrieved 21 July 2014.

Ferguson, Niall (1996). The War of The World: Twentieth-Century Conflict and the Descent of the West (Reprint ed.). Penguin. ISBN 978-0-14-311239-6.

Ferguson, Niall (2009). The War of the World: History's Age of Hatred. Penguin. ISBN 978-0-14-101382-4.

Ginn, Courtney (2013). "Ensuring The Effective Prosecution Of Sexually Violent Crimes In The Bosnian War Crimes Chamber: Applying Lessons From The ICTY". Emory International Law Review 27: 566–601.

Goodman, Walter (3 March 1997). "Women as Victims of the Bosnian War". New York Times. Retrieved 4 August 2014.

Haas, Michael (2013). International Human Rights: A Comprehensive Introduction (2nd ed.). Routledge. ISBN 978-0-415-53820-6.

Hazan, Pierre (2004). Justice in a Time of War: The True Story Behind the International Criminal Tribunal for the Former Yugoslavia. Texas A & M University Press. ISBN 978-1-58544-411-3.

Hewstone, Miles (2009). "Why Neighbors Kill: Prior Intergroup Contact and Ethnic Outgroup Neighbors". In Esses, Victoria M.; Vernon, Richard A. Explaining the Breakdown of Ethnic Relations. Wiley-Blackwell. pp. 61–92. ISBN 978-1-4443-0306-3.

Husejnović, Merima (26 January 2009). "Analysis – Nikacevic: Ten Witnesses Deny Rape Allegations". BIRN (Justice Report). Retrieved 3 August 2014.

Hyndman, Jennifer (2009). "Genocide and Ethnic Cleansing". In Essed, Philomena; Goldberg, David Theo; Kobayashi, Audrey. A Companion to Gender Studies (New ed.). Wiley-Blackwell. pp. 202–211. ISBN 978-1-4051-8808-1.

Ivanišević, Bogdan (2008). The War Crimes Chamber in Bosnia and Herzegovina: From Hybrid to Domestic Court. International Center for Transitional Justice.

Johan Vetlesen, Arne (2005). Evil and Human Agency: Understanding Collective Evildoing. Cambridge University Press. ISBN 978-0-521-67357-0.

Kennedy, Michael D. (2002). Cultural Formations of Postcommunism: Emancipation, Transition, Nation and War. University of Minnesota Press. ISBN 978-0-8166-3857-4.

Kosmidou, Eleftheria Rania (2012). European Civil War Films: Memory, Conflict, and Nostalgia. Routledge. ISBN 978-0-415-52320-2.

LeBor, Adam (2006). "Recently Disturbed Earth". "Complicity with Evil" The United Nations in the Age of Modern Genocide. Yale University Press. ISBN 978-0-300-13514-5.

Lee, John Y. (2000). "Japanese War Criminals on the U.S. Justice Departments "Watchlist" of 3 December 1996: The Legal and Political Background". In Stetz, Margaret D.; Oh, Bonnie B. C. Legacies of the Comfort Women of World War II. M.E. Sharpe. pp. 152–170. ISBN 978-0-7656-0544-3.

Lekha Sriram, Chandra; Martin-Ortega, Olga; Herman, Johanna (2014). War, Conflict and Human Rights: Theory and practice (2nd ed.). Routledge. ISBN 978-0-415-83226-7.

Lončar, Mladen; Medved, Vesna (2006). "Psychological Consequences of Rape on Women in 1991–1995 War in Croatia and Bosnia and Herzegovina". Croatian Medical Journal 1 (47): 67–75. PMC 2080379. PMID 16489699.

Luban, David (2009). International and transnational criminal law. Aspen. ISBN 978-0-7355-6214-1.

MacKinnon, Catharine A. (1994). "Turning Rape into Pornography: Postmodern Genocide". In Stiglmayer, Alexandra. Mass Rape: The War against Women in Bosnia-Herzegovina. Bison Books. pp. 73–187. ISBN 978-0-8032-4239-5.

Malek, Cate (2005). "Reconciliation in Bosnia". Beyond Intractability (University of Colorado). Retrieved 23 July 2014.

Maners, Lynn D. (2000). "Clapping for Serbs: Nationalism and Performance in Bosnia and Herzegovina". In Halpern, Joel M.; Kideckel, David A. Neighbors at War: Anthropological Perspectives on Yugoslav Ethnicity, Culture and History. Pennsylvania State University Press. pp. 302–315. ISBN 978-0-271-01979-6.

May, Larry (2007). War Crimes and Just War (1st ed.). Cambridge University Press. ISBN 978-0-521-69153-6.

McDonald, Gabrielle Kirk; Swaak-Goldman, Olivia (1999). Substantive and Procedural Aspects of International Criminal Law: The Experience of International and National Courts, Documents: 002. Kluwer Law. ISBN 978-90-411-1134-0.

Meron, Theodor (2011). The Making of International Criminal Justice: A View from the Bench: Selected Speeches. Oxford University Press. ISBN 978-0-19-960893-5.

Mojzes, Paul (2011). Balkan Genocides: Holocaust and Ethnic Cleansing in the Twentieth Century. Balkan Genocides: Holocaust and Ethnic Cleansing in the Twentieth Century. ISBN 978-1-4422-0663-2.

Morales, Waltraud Queiser (2001). "Feminization of Global Scarcity and Violence". In Dobkowski, Michael N.; Wallimann, Isidor. On the Edge of Scarcity: Environment, Resources, Population, Sustainability and Conflict (2nd ed.). Syracuse University Press. pp. 173–182. ISBN 978-0-8156-2943-6.

Dombrowski, Nicole A. (2004). Women and War in the Twentieth Century: Enlisted With Or Without Consent. Routledge. p. 333; The apparent uniqueness of the rape directed overwhelmingly against Bosnian-Muslim women as part of a genocidal campaign of "ethnic cleansing". ISBN 978-0-415-97256-7.

Oosthuizen, Gabriël H. (2010). Review of the Sexual Violence Elements of the Judgements of the International Criminal Tribunal for the Former Yugoslavia, the International Criminal ... the Light of Security Council Resolution 18. United Nations. ISBN 978-92-1-137032-4.

Pelinka, Anton; Ronen, Dov (1997). The Challenge of Ethnic Conflict, Democracy and Self-determination in Central Europe. Routledge. ISBN 978-0-7146-4752-4.

Pulver, Andrew (10 February 2012). "In the Land of Blood and Honey – review". The Guardian. Retrieved 4 August 2014.

Ralston, John H.; Finnin, Sarah (2007). "International Law Enforcement Strategies". In Blumenthal, David A.; McCormack, Timothy L. H. The Legacy of Nuremberg: Civilising Influence Or Institutionalised Vengeance?. Brill. pp. 47–68. ISBN 978-90-04-15691-3.

Robinson, Darryl (1998). "Trials, Tribulations, and Triumphs: Major Developments in 1997 at the International Criminal Tribunal for the Former Yugoslavia". In McRae, Donald M. The Canadian Yearbook of International Law (Volume 35 ed.). University of British Columbia Press. pp. 179–213. ISBN 978-0-7748-0679-4.

Sander, Helke (1994). "Prologue". In Stiglmayer, Alexandra. Mass Rape: The War against Women in Bosnia-Herzegovina. Bison Books. pp. xvii–xxiii. ISBN 978-0-8032-4239-5.

Senasi, Deneen (2008). "Signs of Desire: Nationalism, War, and Rape in Titus Andronicus, Savior, and Calling the Ghosts". In Forter, Greg;

Miller, Paul Allen. Desire of the Analysts: Psychoanalysis and Cultural Criticism. State University of New York Press. pp. 99–122. ISBN 978-0-7914-7300-9.

Stiglmayer, Alexandra (1994). "The Rapes in Bosnia-Herzegovina". In Stiglmayer, Alexandra. Mass Rape: The War Against Women in Bosnia-Herzegovina. University of Nebraska Press. pp. 82–169. ISBN 978-0-8032-9229-1.

Skjelsbæk, Inger (2006). "Victim and Survivor: Narrated Social Identities of Women Who Experienced Rape During the War in Bosnia-Herzegovina". Feminism & Psychology (Sage) 16 (4): 373–403. doi:10.1177/0959353506068746.

"Seventh Report on War Crimes in the Former Yugoslavia: Part II". US submission of information to the United Nations Security Council. 1993. Retrieved 27 June 2014.

Simic, Olivera (2014). Regulation of Sexual Conduct in UN Peacekeeping Operations. Springer. ISBN 978-3-642-42785-5.

"Bosnian Serb gets 18 years in killings". Los Angeles Times. 4 July 2009. Retrieved 3 August 2014.

Totten, Samuel; Bartrop, Paul R. (2007). Dictionary of Genocide. ABC-CLIO. ISBN 978-0-313-32967-8.

Henry, Nicola (2010). War and Rape: Law, Memory, and Justice. Routledge. ISBN 978-0-415-56472-4.

Jones, Adam (2006). Genocide: A Comprehensive Introduction. Routledge. ISBN 978-0-415-35384-7.

Leaning, Jennifer; Susan Bartels, and Hani Mowafi (2009). "Sexual Violence during War and Forced Migration". In Susan Forbes Martin, John Tirman. Women, Migration, and Conflict: Breaking a Deadly Cycle. Springer. pp. 173–199. ISBN 978-90-481-2824-2. Cite uses deprecated parameter |coauthors= (help)

Lieberman, Benjamin (2013). The Holocaust and Genocides in Europe (1st ed.). Bloomsbury Academic. ISBN 978-1-4411-9478-7.

Wood, Elisabeth J. (2013). Miranda A.H Horvath, Jessica Woodhams, ed. Handbook on the Study of Multiple Perpetrator Rape: A multidisciplinary response to an international problem. Routledge. ISBN 978-0-415-50044-9.

Sjoberg, Laura; Gentry, Caron E. (2007). Mothers, Monsters, Whores: Women's Violence in Global Politics. Zed Books. ISBN 978-1-84277-866-1.

"Bosnia court jails ex-Serb army commander for 18 years". Reuters. 2009-07-03. Retrieved 2009-07-07.

Saunders, Doug (5 April 2009). "Children born of rape come of age in Bosnia". Globe and Mail. Retrieved 23 July 2014.

Smith-Spark, Laura (8 December 2004). "How did rape become a weapon of war?". British Broadcasting Corporation. Retrieved 29 December 2013.

Van Sliedregt, Elies (2012). Individual Criminal Responsibility in International Law. Oxford University Press. ISBN 978-0-19-956036-3.

Weitsman, Patricia A. (2008). "The Politics of Identity and Sexual Violence: A Review of Bosnia and Rwanda". Human Rights Quarterly 30 (3): 561–578. doi:10.1353/hrq.0.0024.

Waller, James E. (2002). Becoming Evil: How Ordinary People Commit Genocide and Mass Killing. Oxford University Press. ISBN 978-0-19-514868-8.

Walsh, Annelotte (2012). "International Criminal Justice and the Girl Child". In Yarwood, Lisa. Women and Transitional Justice: The Experience of Women as Participants. Lisa Yarwood. pp. 54–74. ISBN 978-0-415-69911-2.

Weitsman, Patricia (2007). "Children Born of War and the Politics of Identity". In Carpenter, Charli. Born of War: Protecting Children of Sexual Violence Survivors in Conflict Zones. Kumarian Press. pp. 110–127. ISBN 978-1-56549-237-0.

Williams, Paul R.; Scharf, Michael P. (1998). "Task Force Statement of the Twentieth Century Fund's Task Force on Apprehending Indicted War Criminals: Meeting the Obligations of Justice". Human Rights (American Bar Association) 3 (25): 17–20. JSTOR 27880109.

Yee, Sienho (2003). "The Doctrine of Command Responsibility". International Crime and Punishment: Selected Issues (Volume 1 ed.). University Press of America. ISBN 978-0-7618-2570-8.

Zappala, Salvatore (2009). "Cases". In Cassese, Antonio. The Oxford Companion to International Criminal Justice. Oxford University Press. pp. 683–685. ISBN 978-0-19-923832-3.

Zuvela, Maja (19 February 2009). "Bosnian Serb jailed for 8 years for wartime rapes". Reuters. Retrieved 3 August 2014.

External links

General

Odjek: Zločin silovanja u Bosni i Hercegovini (Bosnian)

Gendercide Watch - Case Study: Bosnia-Herzegovina

Mass rape - New York Times 1993

Bosnia's rape babies: abandoned by their families, forgotten by the state

Rape: weapon of war

Reports

Orentlicher, Diane (1997). "Sexual Assault Issues Before the War Crimes Tribunal". Human Rights Brief 4 (2): 8–9.

When Everyone is Silent: Reparation for Survivors of Wartime Rape in Republika Srpska in Bosnia and Herzegovina (PDF). Amnesty International (Report). 31 October 2012. EUR 63/012/2012.

Whose Justice? Bosnia and Herzegovina's Women Still Waiting (PDF). Amnesty International (Report). 30 September 2009. EUR 63/006/2009.

Case Study:

Bosnia-Herzegovina

Ratko Mladic and Radovan Karadzic, war criminals

Summary

Atrocities were committed by all sides and against all sectors of the population in Bosnia-Herzegovina between 1992 and 1995. But the Serb strategy of gender-selective mass executions of non-combatant men was the most severe and systematic atrocity inflicted throughout. The war in Bosnia can thus be considered both a genocide against Bosnia's Muslim population, and a gendercide against Muslim men in particular.

The background

The Yugoslav ("Southern Slav") federation, cobbled together from the disintegrated Ottoman Empire after World War I, was torn apart by combined Nazi invasion and ethnic conflict during the Second World War. Indeed, the slaughter of Serbs, Muslims, Croats, and Roma (Gypsies) constituted one of the most genocidal theatres of that war. A partisan movement led by Josip Broz Tito (a Croat) seized power with Allied help, massacred its enemies, and established a comparatively

47

liberal socialist state, creating an atmosphere for a sense of Yugoslav nationhood to flourish (an idea that lives on today in "Cyber-Yugoslavia"). The federation began to unwind after Marshal Tito's death in 1980, with economic crisis and foreign debt speeding the dissolution of the union. A new generation of extreme-nationalist politicians arose to fan the flames of ethnic hatred as a springboard to personal power. In Serbia, President Slobodan Milosevic consolidated his highly authoritarian brand of rule after 1987, imposing a police state on the restive Serb province of Kosovo and its ethnic-Albanian majority in 1989. Franjo Tudjman, meanwhile, won presidential elections in Croatia by reviving the symbolism and rhetoric of the fascist Ustashe, Croatia's Nazi collaborationists, who fifty years earlier had inflicted genocide on the Serbs and Roma within their reach.

While Tudjman and others played an important role in ensuring that the breakup of Yugoslavia would be violent, it was overridingly Milosevic's ambitions of a "Greater Serbia" that sparked the onset of fullscale war in both Croatia and Bosnia-Herzegovina. Using its dominant control over the Yugoslav army, the Serb regime shelled large parts of Croatia into submission in 1991 (including the destruction of the Danube city of Vukovar and the subsequent genocidal massacre: see below). The Bosnian government, almost defenseless, desperately sought to stay out of the widening conflict. But the following year, in Spring 1992, Milosevic -- in alliance with Radovan Karadzic's breakaway Bosnian Serbs -- launched the genocidal and gendercidal "ethnic cleansing" of those parts of Bosnia intended for "Greater Serbia." Sarajevo's time-honoured ethnic harmony was shattered by a protracted Serb siege. Meanwhile, the outside world dithered ineffectually, imposing an arms embargo on the Bosnian Muslims equal to the one it imposed on the well-armed Serbs. Europe's worst conflict since the Second World War was underway, and the military imbalance placed Milosevic's genocidal ambitions within reach.

The Gendercide

In the light of long-established and heavily "gendered" strategies of intercommunal conflict in the Balkans, it was hardly surprising that the gender-selective massacre of non-combatant males would emerge as the dominant and most severe atrocity inflicted on the civilian population in the modern Balkans wars. Regardless of their often-atrocious maltreatment of other population groups (including the destruction of entire cities and the mass rape of women), Serb forces and to a lesser extent Croats and Muslims, concentrated their attention systematically on "battle-age" men. As the Bosnian Prime Minister Hasan Muratovic described the Serb strategy in 1996, "Wherever they [the Serbs] captured people, they either detained or killed all the males from 18 to 55 [years old]. It has never happened that the men of that age arrived across the front-line." Citing Muratovic's comment, Mark Danner summarized the Serbs' modus operandi as follows:

1. Concentration. Surround the area to be cleansed and after warning the resident Serbs, often they are urged to leave or are at least told to mark their houses with white flags, intimidate the target population with

artillery fire and arbitrary executions and then bring them out into the streets.

2. Decapitation. Execute political leaders and those capable of taking their places: lawyers, judges, public officials, writers, professors.

3. Separation. Divide women, children, and old men from men of "fighting age" : sixteen years to sixty years old.

4. Evacuation. Transport women, children, and old men to the border, expelling them into a neighboring territory or country.

5. Liquidation. Execute "fighting age" men, dispose of bodies.

All of the largest atrocities of the Balkans war were variations on this gendercidal theme, targeting males almost exclusively, and for the most part "battle-age" males. The five worst acts of mass killing in the modern Balkans wars were also the worst in Europe since the killing of tens of thousands of disarmed enemy men by Tito's partisan forces in 1945-46. At Vukovar in November 1991, between 200 and 300 Croatian men, "mostly lightly wounded soldiers and hospital workers," were pulled out of the hospital surroundings -- some with the catheters still dangling from their arms : executed, and buried en masse outside city limits. (See Stover and Peress, The Graves: Srebrenica and Vukovar.)

A panel from Joe Sacco's memorable work, Safe Area Gorazde

(link to ordering information for Sacco's book).

Panel from Joe Sacco's 'Safe Area Gorazde'

The story of Vlasic (Ugar Gorge) is that of another ruthless act of gender-selective mass killing. On 21 August 1992, a convoy of prisoners from the Serb-run Trnopolje concentration camp were driven to Muslim and Croat territory. En route, men were separated from women, driven off in separate buses, and executed at the edge of the ravine. Some 200-250 men are believed to have died.

But neither Vukovar nor the Ugar Gorge could hold a candle to a more obscure slaughter -- at Brcko during the Serb offensive of 1992. Although much about the incident remains shadowy, Brcko, a strategic "choke point" on the Drina River, appears to have been the target of a systematic gender-selective slaughter that strongly foreshadowed the nightmare at Srebrenica three years later. Mark Danner, who has investigated what little is publicly known about the events, summarizes them as follows:

During the late spring and early summer of 1992, some three thousand Muslims .... were herded by Serb troops into an abandoned warehouse, tortured, and put to death. A U.S. intelligence satellite orbiting over the former Yugoslavia photographed part of the slaughter. "They have photos of trucks going into Brcko with bodies standing upright, and pictures of trucks coming out of Brcko carrying bodies lying horizontally, stacked like cordwood," an investigator working outside the U.S. government who has seen the photographs told us. ... The photographs remain unpublished to this day. (Danner, "Bosnia: The Great Betrayal," New York Review of Books, 26 March 1998.)

The vast majority of mass killings and gender-selective slaughters between 1991 and 1994 were smaller in magnitude, and went virtually unrecorded. The best place to find accounts of them, in English at least, is the Helsinki Watch/Human Rights Watch report, War Crimes in Bosnia-Herzegovina. The litany of atrocities in a narrow stretch of Volume II alone makes clear the pervasiveness and systematic character of the gendercide in Bosnia-Herzegovina, in a way that the more epic mass killings perhaps do not:

In my village, about 180 men were killed. The army put all men in the center of the village. After the killing, the women took care of the bodies and identified them. The older men buried the bodies. (Trnopolje)

We were met by the Cetniks [Serb paramilitaries], who were separating women and children from the men. Many of the men were killed on the spot -- mostly over old, private disputes. The rest of us were put on buses and they started to beat us. (Kozarac)

The army came to the village that day. They took us from our houses. The men were beaten. The army came in on trucks and started shooting at the men and killing them. (Prnovo)

The army took most of the men and killed them. There were bodies everywhere. (Rizvanovici)

The shooting started at about 4:00 p.m., but we were surrounded and could not escape. They [Serb troops] finally entered the village at 8:00 p.m. and immediately began setting houses on fire, looking for men and executing them. When they got to our house, they ordered us to come out with hands raised above our heads, including the children. There were four men among us, and they shot them in front of us. We were screaming, and the children cried as we were forced to walk on. I saw another six men killed nearby. (Skelani)

Our men had to hide. My husband was with us, but hiding. I saw my uncle being beaten on July 25 when there was a kind of massacre. The Serbs were searching for arms. Three hundred men were killed that day. (Carakovo)

We came out of the shelter. They were looking for men. They got them all together. We saw them beating the men. We heard the sounds of the shooting. One man survived the executions. They killed his brother and father. Afterwards the women buried the men. (Biscani)

The crowning act of gendercide in the Balkans wars -- at least until "Operation Horseshoe" in Kosovo in 1999 -- came at Srebrenica between July 12 and 17, 1995. After the atrocities of 1992 and further fighting in 1993, Srebrenica had been declared one of five "safe areas" under UN protection. Tens of thousands of desperate Muslims sought protection there. Despite privations and squalor, the safety held -- until July 1995, when Serb forces overran the enclave. As Dutch U.N. troops and the international community looked on, the Serbs separated the men, most of them elderly and infirm, from the children and women. While the other members of the community were bused to safety in Muslim-held territory, thousands of Srebrenica's men were taken out to open fields, executed, and buried in mass graves. Thousands of other unarmed men were rounded up and hunted down in nearby forests, in what Serb commander Ratko Mladic called a "feast" of mass killing.

How many died?

"As of December 1994," writes Sabrina Ramet in Balkan Babel (p. 267), "between 200,000 and 400,000 people had died since June 1991 as a result of the war between Serbs and non-Serbs, and at least 2.7 million people had been reduced to refugees. An estimated 20,000-50,000 Bosnian Muslim WOMEN had been RAPED by Bosnian Serb soldiers in a SYSTEMATIC campaign of humiliation and psychological terror." Most authorities, while accepting that the death-toll from the Bosnian conflict alone reached six figures, would tend towards the lower end of Ramet's casualty estimate. But to this must be added the further slaughter during the "endgame" of the war in mid-1995, including the gendercidal massacre at Srebrenica and the Croat invasion of the Serb-held Krajina region later in the summer.

No reliable statistics exist for the number of male versus female casualties in the Bosnian or Croatian wars. All members of the civilian population suffered in the protracted and bloody sieges of cities such as Vukovar and Sarajevo. But the overwhelming weight of testimony and recorded evidence suggests a heavy preponderance of "battle-age" males among the dead -- probably over 80 percent. One clue can be gleaned from the lists of missing persons from the Bosnian conflict. The International Committee of the Red Cross has noted that "the majority of missing persons [in Bosnia-Herzegovina] are men ... Of the approximately 18,000 persons registered by the ICRC in Bosnia-Herzegovina as still missing in connection with the armed conflict that ended there in 1995, 92% are men and 8% are women." (ICRC, "The Impact of Armed Conflict on Women", 6 March 2001.) This apparent disproportion, combined with the systematic gender-selective strategies pursued in the individual massacres and "ethnic cleansing" campaigns, warrants the designation of Bosnia-Herzegovina as one of the worst gendercides in recent decades. Especially in 1992-93, atrocities were also inflicted in the brutal concentration camps operated by the Serbs (e.g., Omarska, Trnopolje), and to a lesser extent by the Croats (Dretelj). The inmates of these camps were overwhelmingly Muslim males (95 percent or more); many thousands died from torture, beatings, and summary executions.

Who is responsible?

Bosnia War Crime

Although crimes have been committed by all sides in the Balkans conflict, the vast majority of the mass killings and other atrocities were inflicted by the Yugoslav regime of Slobodan Milosevic. Milosevic himself now numbers among those indicted by the International Criminal Tribunal for the Former Yugoslavia (ICTY), on the basis of his genocidal actions in Kosovo. He is presently the only sitting head of state to be so indicted. Four top aides were indicted alongside him. Among Milosevic's key co-conspirators is his wife, Mirjana Markovic, a leading party ideologue. (Milošević resigned the Yugoslav presidency amid demonstrations, following the disputed presidential election of 24 September 2000. He was arrested by Yugoslav federal authorities on 31 March 2001 on suspicion of corruption, abuse of power, and embezzlement. The initial investigation into Milošević faltered for lack of evidence, prompting the Serbian Prime Minister Zoran Đinđić to extradite him to the International Criminal Tribunal for the former Yugoslavia (ICTY) to stand trial for charges of war crimes instead. At the outset of the trial Milošević denounced the Tribunal as illegal because it had not been established with the consent of the United Nations General Assembly; therefore he refused to appoint counsel for his defence. Milošević conducted his own defence in the five-year-long trial, which ended without a verdict when he died in his prison cell in The Hague on 11 March 2006. Milošević, who suffered from heart ailments and hypertension, died of a heart attack. The Tribunal denied any responsibility for Milošević's death, and stated that he had refused to take prescribed medicines and medicated himself instead. In February 2007, the International Court of Justice (ICJ) ruled separately in the Bosnian Genocide Case that there was no evidence linking Serbia and Milošević to genocide committed by Bosnian Serbs in the Bosnian war. However, the Court did find that Milošević and others in Serbia had committed a breach of the Genocide Convention by failing to prevent the genocide from occurring and for not cooperating with the ICTY in punishing the perpetrators of the genocide, in particular General Ratko Mladić, and for violating its obligation to comply with the provisional measures ordered by the Court).

The Yugoslav power structure is extensively penetrated by criminal and paramilitary elements, most notably those under the control of Zeljko Raznatovic ("Arkan") and Vojislav Seselj. Both of these paramilitary leaders were deeply involved in the ground-level killing at the major massacre sites. Radovan Karadzic, President of the self-declared "Republika Srpska" (the Serb statelet in Bosnia-Herzegovina), has also been indicted on war-crimes charges. He was intimately involved in planning and preparing the genocidal actions against the Muslim population of Bosnia. On 24 March 2016, he was found guilty of genocide in Srebrenica, war crimes and crimes against humanity, 10 of the 11 charges in total and sentenced to 40 years' imprisonment. His top general, Ratko Mladic, supervised the gendercide at Srebrenica and numerous other acts of mass killing, and is also under indictment. Mladic's trial in the ICTY is still ongoing.

One must not overlook the men and occasionally women who slaughtered the defenseless victims and buried them in the mass graves, or killed them in their houses and streets. Again, although extreme nationalism was evident in Croatia, Bosnia-Herzegovina, and Kosovo, it is the ordinary citizens of Serbia who have overridingly supported their regime in its campaign to build "Greater Serbia" over the graves of Muslims, Croats, and Kosovars.

The aftermath

The slaughter at Srebrenica, which seemed to mark the apogee of "Greater Serbia," was quickly followed by its demise. A Croat-Muslim alliance, now rearmed with tacit U.S. assistance, went on the offensive. "On August 4 [1995], with clear U.S. backing, Croatia's army attacked and overran Knin, the symbolic capital of the rebel Serbs who, at the instigation of Slobodan Milosevic and the Yugoslav army, had seized a quarter of Croatia's territory and driven out their Croat neighbors in 1990 and 1991. Within hours, the tide of the wars in Yugoslavia had shifted. The rebel Serbs' leaders abandoned the civilian Serb population in Croatia. The Croatian army sent tens of thousands of these Serbs fleeing across the Croatian border into Serb-held districts in Bosnia." (Sudetic, Blood and Vengeance, p. 324.) Many thousands of Serbs, especially the elderly and infirm, were killed by Croat forces in these new vengeful "cleansings." Milosevic and his Bosnian Serb allies were forced to the negotiating table. In November 1995, at Dayton, Ohio, they signed a peace treaty with Muslim and Croat representatives that saw Bosnia-Herzegovina formally preserved as an independent country, though with clear areas of predominance for Serbs, Muslims, and Croats. The pact was secured by 60,000 NATO peacekeepers -- but Milosevic's "Greater Serbia" dream remained. It would turn its attentions next to the territory it had first focused upon -- Kosovo, with its rebellious ethnic-Albanian majority. The result was a renewed bout of "ethnic cleansing" and gendercide in the Balkans, in 1998-99.

As was reported by Ian Traynor (12 July 2005), "Muslims regain Srebrenica – for one day" in The Guardian (London). "Truly scenes from hell, written on the darkest pages of human history", was the opinion of Judge Riad in November 1995 when he indicted both, Karadzic and Mladic for genocide in Srebrenica at the war crimes tribunal in The Hague. Thousands of men executed and buried in mass graves, hundreds of men buried alive, men and women mutilated and slaughtered, children killed before their mothers' eyes, a grandfather forced to eat the liver of his own grandson."

Today, the vast majority of armed conflicts occur within a State's borders. Such internal conflicts have a devastating impact upon civilian populations. With respect to civilian women, there used to be a perceived security - a sense that as a woman and especially as a mother one would be spared the excesses of warfare. Recent and present conflicts show that this perception often does not correspond to reality.

On the contrary, women are targeted precisely because they are women. For example, they are raped in order to humiliate, frighten and defeat the "enemy" group to which they belong.

Over the past two years, the **International Committee of the Red Cross** (**ICRC**) has carried out a study aimed at improving its understanding of the specific impact that armed conflict has on women. This study, the final report of which is nearing completion, investigates the needs of women in war, the protection accorded to women by international humanitarian law, and ICRC activities on behalf of women in our worldwide operations. Thanks to lessons from past and current experiences the ICRC can better understand the ways in which women are affected by armed conflict and improve the quality, relevance and impact of its services. The study is also intended to motivate all others involved in conflict situations - whether directly or indirectly - to seek ways of preventing and, when necessary, alleviating the suffering of women in war.

Study process

The systematic collection of information began in 1998 and continued through the year 2000.

ICRC field delegations were requested to provide periodic reports regarding activities carried out on behalf of women. Visits were made to 14 delegations to gather information and hold discussions with ICRC personnel. During these visits, interviews were arranged with women affected by armed conflict in camps for displaced persons, prisons, hospitals and orthopaedic centres, and also with beneficiaries of ICRC programmes and with women's organizations. Information was gathered from ICRC personnel returning from the field, and also from ICRC publications, documents and training materials.

Furthermore, valuable information was provided by war-affected women themselves in the context of the People on War project marking the 50th anniversary of the 1949 Geneva Conventions.

Key findings of the study, or eight themes for the eighth of March relating to the impact of armed conflict on women

(1) Displacement. As members of the civilian population, women and girls can be subjected to innumerable acts of violence during armed conflicts. Increased insecurity and fear of attack often cause women and their dependants to flee, and it is frequently pointed out that women and children constitute the majority (usually estimated at 80%) of the world's internally displaced persons and refugees. They also flee because their menfolk have fled, are detained, or are missing in connection with the hostilities, or because the men have sent them away following the breakdown of traditional protection mechanisms. The impact of the displacement of women is enormous. They flee into uncertainty and often into danger, as they have to fend for themselves and support their dependants with few resources or belongings.

(2) Security. Women invariably have to bear increased responsibility for their children and elderly relatives - and the wider community - in the absence of their menfolk. They often choose not to flee the fighting or the threat of hostilities because they and their families believe that the very fact that they are women and mothers will make them safe from the warring parties. They therefore stay to protect their families and provide for them. But the absence of their men and the general instability and lawlessness that characterize many of today's conflicts heighten the insecurity of the women caught up in these situations, and exacerbate the breakdown of the traditional support mechanisms upon which the community - women especially - previously relied.

(3) Sexual violence. Rape, forced prostitution, sexual slavery and forced impregnation are all criminal means and methods of warfare that have attracted more and more attention in recent years, mainly because of the widespread reporting of such acts in recent conflicts. Sexual violence has in fact always been used against women and girls - and to a lesser extent against men and boys - as a form of torture used to degrade, intimidate and ultimately defeat and chase away targeted populations. Sexual violence, including rape, is brutal and terrifying for its victims and the whole community. It constitutes a serious violation of international humanitarian law.

(4) Missing persons. One of the most harrowing consequences of armed conflicts, which continues long after the hostilities are over, is that people go missing. The majority of missing persons are men, which

leaves large numbers of women seeking news of their fate. Of the approximately 18,000 persons registered by the ICRC in Bosnia-Herzegovina as still missing in connection with the armed conflict that ended there in 1995, 92% are men and 8% are women.

The inability to ascertain the fate of loved ones and to mourn and bury those who have died has a devastating effect on the survivors of war and on their ability to cope. The search for missing relatives drags on long after armed conflicts have ended, and can be a lasting impediment to the process of reconciliation. Furthermore, widows and relatives of missing men are often left without any entitlement to land, homes, inheritances, social assistance or pensions, or even the right to sign contracts.

(5) Detention. Statistics on detention and internment during hostilities highlight the differences between the fates of women and men in situations of armed conflict. Civilian men are far more likely to be perceived as combatants or potential combatants, and consequently to be detained or interned, than women. In 1999, for example, the ICRC visited more than 225,000 detainees around the world, fewer than 10,000 of whom were women and girls. Although women are less frequently detained than men in relation to hostilities, their menfolk's detention still has an enormous impact on them, especially when they are left to head their household and support dependent family members - a role for which many women are ill-prepared and which is made even more difficult by the insecurity and deprivation due to war.

(6) Access to medical care. Armed conflicts seriously affect the health of an entire population - women, men and children. The insecure environment prevailing in areas of conflict or internal disturbance makes it difficult for civilians to reach health services and receive appropriate medical care and medicines. Local medical services and infrastructure can be severely disrupted and even partly or completely destroyed. Reproductive health care is vital to save lives and prevent and reduce illnesses and disabilities due to complications during pregnancy and labour, and after giving birth. In wartime, it is often difficult for women to obtain access to specialist medical services, such as reproductive health care, when traditional systems of medical support of any sort may barely be functioning. In addition to obtaining care for themselves, women have an important role in promoting and maintaining the health of their family and community. They know, or can be taught, how to prevent illnesses and care for sick family members and should be supported and assisted in these efforts.

(7) Access to food and other assistance. In situations of armed conflict, the civilian population - women, men and children - may not have the means to ensure their own survival. When men take up arms, flee, become disabled, go missing, are detained, or die, the impact on women can be dramatic. They face the heavy burden of taking over the role of head of household and providing for their own needs and those of their family. Certain tasks traditionally done by men can be difficult for women to carry out because of social and cultural barriers, or lack of skills. Moreover, the insecurity resulting from the hostilities restricts their mobility. Conflict also exposes women to the dangers of mines and unexploded ordnance, and to the risk of attack and sexual violence.

Women should be involved in the planning, implementation and evaluation of assistance programmes set up on their behalf to ensure that the assistance provided meets their needs, priorities and cultural requirements, and that it actually reaches the intended beneficiaries.

(8) International humanitarian law.   International humanitarian law protects women when:

they are active combatants, by laying down limitations on permissible means and methods of warfare;

they are captured, sick or wounded combatants;

they are civilians not taking an active part in the hostilities.

This protection is enshrined in the four Geneva Conventions of 1949 and their two Additional Protocols of 1977 and in a number of other instruments. Women are afforded both general protection - i.e., on the same basis as men - and special protection reflecting their particular needs as women. Women who are not, or no longer, taking part in hostilities are protected against the effects of the fighting and also against abusive treatment by the parties to hostilities. Women are entitled to humane treatment, respect for their life and physical integrity, and to live free from torture, ill-treatment, acts of violence and harassment. They are specially protected against attack, in particular against rape, enforced prostitution and any form of indecent assault. Such acts are prohibited. (Cf. Fourth Geneva Convention, Art. 27(2), and Additional Protocol I, Arts 75 and 76.)

The special protection for women also concerns their conditions of detention or internment, for example by providing that they shall have separate sleeping quarters and sanitary facilities from male detainees or internees. Their specific needs as pregnant women or nursing mothers as members of the civilian population or as detained combatants are also recognized and protected by international humanitarian law.

The ad hoc International Criminal Tribunals for the former Yugoslavia and Rwanda are important developments in the realization of more effective mechanisms for enforcing international humanitarian law. For example, the fact that rape and other forms of sexual violence in armed conflict have been prosecuted as war crimes is a major step forward in the fight against impunity. The resulting International Criminal Court (ICC or ICCt) is an intergovernmental organization and international tribunal that sits in The Hague in the Netherlands. The ICC has the jurisdiction to prosecute individuals for the international crimes of genocide, crimes against humanity, and war crimes. The ICC is intended to complement existing national judicial systems and it may therefore only exercise its jurisdiction when certain conditions are met, such as when national courts are unwilling or unable to prosecute criminals or when the United Nations Security Council or individual states refer investigations to the Court. The ICC began functioning on 1 July 2002, the date that the Rome Statute entered into force. The Rome Statute is a multilateral treaty which serves as the ICC's foundational and governing document. States which become party to the Rome Statute, for example by ratifying it, become member states of the ICC. Currently, there are 124 states which are party to the Rome Statute and therefore members of the ICC.

Conclusion

The fact that violations of international humanitarian law do occur does not mean that this body of law is inadequate. There are rules on permissible means and methods of warfare to protect women, men and children not taking an active part in the hostilities. The fact that women have to bear so much of the tragic burden of hostilities is not primarily because of any shortcomings in the rules protecting them, but because those rules are not observed.

One of the main reasons that the civilian population fails now more than ever to receive the assistance and protection that international humanitarian law affords them is that humanitarian organizations like the ICRC are not given access to areas where the worst fighting is taking place, and the civilian sick and wounded are denied relief offered on their behalf.

Rapid and unimpeded access must be granted to humanitarian organizations so that they can provide assistance and protection to persons affected by armed conflict. Humanitarian relief activities are carried out without any adverse distinction, in accordance with international law.

The plight of civilian women in war is often linked to the fate of the menfolk in their household and community. In other words, such misfortunes as attacks on undefended households and women, rape as a means of attacking the "enemy" population, the displacement of women and their dependants, etc., occur in part at least because of the absence of the men.

To say this is not to deny that women face terrible hardships in armed conflict or that they have their own specific needs and vulnerabilities. On the contrary, it is to recognize that the fate of civilian women can be improved if humanitarian law is fully implemented and respected with regard to combatants and non-combatants, be they male or female.

It is important to set right the notion that women are "vulnerable" and "victims". Women are politicians, community leaders, partners in assistance operations in their communities, and activists for reconstruction, reconciliation and peace. They are also actively engaged in the fighting as combatants or in support roles in the armed forces. Women are not necessarily vulnerable and victims, although many women have been made particularly vulnerable by war.

International Women's Day is an occasion to commemorate the courage, resilience and strength of women. Women display tremendous resourcefulness in the coping mechanisms they have developed as survivors of wars, as participants in humanitarian programmes and as heads of households. One of the greatest challenges for the humanitarian community is to improve the lot of women, who should be better supported, protected and assisted when confronted by war.

On March 8, the ICRC called for the general and special protection to which women are entitled by international humanitarian law to become a reality in each and every armed conflict in the world. Improved protection of women in situations of armed conflict can be achieved through better implementation and respect of existing international humanitarian law and other international norms. Everyone must be made responsible for improving the plight of women in times of conflict. This is not a "pipe dream", but an obligation - a commitment made and enshrined in law which must be upheld.

Based on the opinions above-stated and the preponderance and gravity of opinions that have provided sufficient arguments and concluded from the organized, and systematic nature of the mass rapes of the female Bosniak (Bosnian Muslim) population, lucidly and soundly discern that these rapes were a part of a larger campaign of genocide and that the VRS were carrying out a policy of genocidal rape against the Bosnian Muslim ethnic group.

Hence, the paragraph below is again repeated by reproducing in its entirety:

The International Criminal Tribunal for the former Yugoslavia (ICTY) declared that "systematic rape", and "sexual enslavement" in time of war was a crime against humanity, second only to the war crime of genocide. Although the ICTY did not treat the mass rapes as genocide, many scholars such as Becirevic, Cohen, Boose, Johan Vetlesen etc. have provided sufficient arguments and concluded from the organized, and systematic nature of the mass rapes of the female Bosniak (Bosnian Muslim) population, that these rapes were a part of a larger campaign of genocide and that the VRS were carrying out a policy of genocidal rape against the Bosnian Muslim ethnic group. Utmost due respect is given to the decision of the ICTY.

Photo of a Bosniak/Bosnian Muslim woman who was repeatedly and brutally raped by Serbs in the eastern Bosnian town of Foca near Srebrenica. The Serbs employed a policy of systematic rapes against Bosniak women and underage girls during the Bosnian Genocide (1992-95), forcibly impregnating them to bear the so called 'Serb' children.

www.ingramcontent.com/pod-product-compliance
Lightning Source LLC
Chambersburg PA
CBHW070243190526
45169CB00001B/292